Advance Praise for

The Gift of Taking

"My heart cried with joy as I read your book. Words that come from the heart enter the heart. You have done a most wonderful job at expressing your experiences and insights, so valuable for those who wish to move forward in life. You give us keys and insights to see that which the Creator is constantly giving us. As you aptly point out, it is only waiting for us to take it."

—RABBI YOSEF YITZCHOK SEREBRYANSKI
Author, lecturer and founder of
The Center for Revelations, Brooklyn, New York

"This book is required reading for doctors and anyone challenged with cancer or any illness. It gives patients powerful tools for participating in their own healing process and it gives physicians an encouraging paradigm for hope and success. It complements virtually every type of treatment for facilitating wellness."

—HOWARD MARC SAUL, D.O.
Assistant Professor of Obstetrics and Gynecology
Director of Gynecological Oncology
The Center for Cancer, Cherry Hill, New Jersey

"Jill Kahn has taken an almost impossible mission: to convince women—our most endlessly giving populace—that they have a right, indeed duty, to *take*. In *The Gift of Taking*, Kahn shares an astonishing Dictation given to her by the Universe, leading her and us into an enchanting new realm of thinking, surviving, balancing, and thriving."

—LAURA SZABO-COHEN
Author of *Disaster Blasters, Food No Matter What,* and *Mama Says*

"A different yet powerful approach to personal fulfillment and relationship. Dr. Jill's book shows you how taking care of yourself helps to take care of those around you. She defines a new, easier way of relating to yourself and to everybody else in your life."

—KATHY WOMACK
Former Executive Producer, CNN

"We see the signs but we pretend they will go away. Then one day the signs become so overwhelming that our bodies have no choice but to recognize them and act—or cease to act, when the signs will no longer matter. It seemed as if I had reached the end of the line. Dr. Jill gave me insight and strength . . . and life. She not only captures the spirit of abundance in her book The Gift of Taking—she embodies it."

—HESHIE SEGAL
President and Co-Founder of What If,
a nonprofit organization dedicated to the enhancement
of educational and life experiences of youth.
Professional speaker, trainer, writer, designer, teacher and business owner

"Dr. Jill writes a powerful book that shows us the power that lies within ourselves that will work the miracles that we want and need in our individual lives. A must-read for everyone who has ever looked to others to perform their miracles!"

—DIANA NIGHTINGALE
Author, international speaker and CEO of Keys Publishing, Inc.

"*The Gift of Taking* provides the ultimate definition for the modern concept of extreme self-care. This is master coaching at its best—facilitating the autonomy of independence simultaneously creating uncommon closeness."

—MICHELLE L. CASTO
Whole Life coach
Author of *Get Smart! About Modern Romantic Relationships*
and *Get Smart! About Modern Career Development*

"Be prepared for the 'Olympics' of transformation and change with this trainer of mind and body! Dr. Jill holds nothing back in cheerleading you on to be the best you can be. Her book should be in the hands of every person, physically challenged or not, who wants to rise to their highest level of body and soul performance."

—MICHAEL McKELLER
Physically challenged adventurer, professional speaker and writer.
Creator and host of television show *Extreme Mike*,
an Emmy award-nominated show, using; extreme sports and adventures to illustrate how a
proper attitude can allow anyone to overcome adversities and accept challenges.

"Certainly a challenging and exciting book. Although I have read many writings, I could barely put this one down. An equally powerful book for both men and women!"

—DR. MICHAEL J. DUCKETT
Author of *Breaking the Money Barriers*, self-made multi-millionaire,
President and CEO of Dynamic Consulting & Training,
dedicated to helping individuals and groups find
the path of least resistance to financial independence

"Jill Kahn's story of healing is remarkable. I experienced her ability to guide people into their healing myself when I was diagnosed with breast cancer two years ago. I am cancer free. This book is a must-read for all those on a similar journey."

—REV. SYDNEY MAGILL-LINDQUIST
Associate Minister Unity North Atlanta and
Minister Unity of Gainesville, Georgia

"Dr. Jill's *The Gift of Taking* is an amazing book that encourages your mind to stretch into an entirely new way of thinking. She presents profound solutions, in the most powerful unique ways, making everyday dilemmas seem easier."

—JAMES WERMERT
CEO Zephyr Group Enterprises
Harvard MBA

The Gift of Taking

Honor Yourself First …
All Else Will Follow

~

Dr. Jill Kahn

Published and distributed in the United States by:

IMPRESSIONS Publishing
P.O. Box 71264
Marietta, GA 30007-1264
www.drjillkahn.com • email: info@drjillkahn.com

Publisher's Cataloging-in-Publication
(Provided by Quality Books, Inc.)

Kahn, Jill
    The gift of taking : honor yourself first -- all else
will follow / Jill Kahn. -- 1st ed.
    p. cm.
    ISBN 0-9711157-4-5

    1. Self-actualization (Psychology) 2. Change
(Psychology) 3. Mind and body. 4. Holistic medicine.
5. Self-help techniques. I. Title.

BF637.S4K35 2001   158.1
                QBI01-700654

First Printing July 2001

Printed in the United States of America

To Our World

and

*To my loving husband, Danny,
and my two beautiful children,
Andy and Julia—
the most treasured gifts of my life*

∼

*May life always be filled
with constant reminders of
all your blessings,
as we grow and learn together.*

Contents

One Realization

left an everlasting impression
within my soul . . .
and my life was never the same.

Then God said,

It's time to share!
Overflow this message.
Our world is ready to hear it.

An Open Invitation

~

You are cordially invited
to accompany Dr. Jill
on a life~changing six~day
spiritual adventure

~

Please extend this invitation to others
as we continue to live in gratitude
for a life well~shared.

The Grand Opening

As a Miracle of Nature,
You are Born to Succeed!

I extend my hand with gratitude, thanking you for accommodating the divine. Your sacred soul has chosen to enter into the world for one reason. It's hungry! Its sole intent is to grow and learn. Your purpose is to fill your soul up by adding new dimension and meaning to its essence. As you saturate your soul with experiences, do not fear the pain or the stretch. These lessons create openings for sacred gifts to come pouring in, increasing your value and worth. Honor yourself first and all else will follow . . .

~

There you are, gazing into the looking glass of your life. You may be sighing, realizing that what's shining back is not at all what you had hoped for. Something's missing, yet perhaps you haven't figured out what that is. You are not alone. I am witnessing an overwhelming epidemic in our world of people who have forgotten how to honor and take care of themselves.

I look around and see a world filled with people who say they don't feel good enough, smart enough, or rich enough. People come to me always wishing: *if only* I could win the lottery; *if only* I could lose weight; *if only* I could find my soul mate; *if only* I could be more successful; *if only* I were healthier . . . *then* I would be happy. Without realizing it, they are lost in a wishing well of *if onlys*. If only someone or something on the outside could fill them up on the inside.

We are born to succeed and excel. Why, then, are my days filled with patients literally handing me their tired, wounded minds, bodies and souls, saying, "Help me"? They come to me with emptiness and questions, trying to remember how to capture their lives once again and reclaim the fulfillment that's rightfully theirs. Ready to delve deeper, I prayed:

Please help me. How can I help these people on an even higher level?

As my soul asked, the floodgates opened and the answers came pouring in!

PREPARATION OF THE SOUL

To be ready to receive and understand the messages to come, I had to be prepared. I learned my lessons along the way—a lifetime's worth of lessons. Twenty years and thousands of patients have helped guide my soul to be ready to unfold the hidden mysteries within that reflect our universe and our lives. I feel blessed.

People come from far and wide to hear my story—to hear that "anything is possible." For the first time, hope and belief enter the minds of those who have given up, those who have lost their passion or believe there are no other choices for them, or those who just can't figure it out. These are people who are ill, whose emotions are out of control, or whose souls are in distress because they've lost their spiritual connections. Now they are ready to learn how they can turn their lives around and take responsibility for their healing. That's when I enter the picture.

WHO I AM AND WHAT I REPRESENT TO THIS WORLD

I am Dr. Jill Kahn, and I am a catalyst of health and healing. I have devoted my life to helping people rise up out of emotional deprivation and debilitating physical illnesses into overflowing, abundant lives. I teach by example. I am living proof, as are the people I have helped, that we *do* have choices and we *can* take charge of our health and our lives.

I passionately threw myself into my work as a chiropractic physician twenty years ago, but realized quickly that the origins of illness go much deeper than the physical. Along with my training, I use my intuitive gifts to reconnect people with their spirit and purpose so that they can achieve true health once again. I am blessed with the ability to help patients see through their problems and blocks, enabling them to understand what their bodies are telling them and the truth of who they are. As my patients participate with me, they learn how to make nurturing choices to transform their lives. They remember how to fill themselves up and thrive.

LOOKING THROUGH FRESH EYES

Right now, in this moment, as you look at all your challenges, you may be thinking, *There must be more to life.* Wouldn't it change your perspective if you knew without a shadow of a doubt that your difficulties are really ways of stretching your soul to your next level of greatness? Wouldn't you be grateful if you knew these trying lessons are powerful enough to expand your spirit to receive more of what you want in life? Wouldn't you relax if you knew you were really being divinely guided, even if it didn't make sense at the time?

GIFTS THAT COME IN UGLY PACKAGES

In hindsight, it's easy to see that all of our life lessons are gifts. They are all preparation for our soul's growth. Some gifts will present themselves in lovely, shiny wrapping paper with a big, beautiful bow. Then there are those that come in ugly packages we don't want to unwrap. I've had many wonderful gifts in my life, but there were quite a few early on that I wanted to stamp RETURN TO SENDER! My strong sense of faith is what made it all easier: I have always trusted that everything happens for a reason and that I was being led.

In chiropractic school, I discovered a lump in my breast. I wasn't alarmed, but a friend was. He handed me a book on healing cancer naturally and insisted that I get tested. It turned out to be a swollen lymph node, so I didn't "need" the book. However, I was still drawn to it without knowing why. I listened to my gut feelings and began reading it. I read more and more—everything I could get my hands on about cancer and the body's way of healing itself naturally. The philosophies I read about were in direct alignment with my own way of life. The lessons were valuable in my practice. But it wasn't until ten years later that I discovered the real reason behind all that preparation.

~

In 1990, my fifty-five-year-old father, Stanley, called in a panic. He had been diagnosed with malignant adenocarcinoma, a very aggressive lung cancer. Unanimously, the oncologists predicted that with prescribed treatments, he had only one to two years to live—at the most. That was one "gift" I didn't want to open.

I was heartsick and had to call upon everything I had inside me to be strong. I could feel my father resigning himself and accepting his "fate." He was settling. That was *not* OK with me!

He had spent his whole life willingly sacrificing for his children, giving relentlessly to make sure we had it all. He had put all three of us through medical and chiropractic schools. I sensed his hopelessness and resignation. He had accepted that his life was over and his purpose was complete now that his children were set on their life paths. My tears came. I told him I wanted him to have fun for himself. He was worth it! I wanted my children to know their wonderful grandfather. He was touched. I could sense a longing behind his words. His mind and his heart were not speaking the same language. His mind had flatlined, but his heart still held a ray of hope. "Is that the way you feel, Dad?" I asked. He said, "Yes . . . but there's nothing else to do."

GOING FOR A MIRACLE

I replied fervently, "But there *is* more we can do!" I knew right then why I had read all those books on healing cancer. It was crystal clear: I was to share with others how to create a more balanced approach to health. My father wanted to hear more. I told him, "Dad, you can beat this! I know you can! You are going to be fine!" With this new information, his mind came alive to possibilities. He trusted his instincts and went against the advice of his doctors. He decided against chemotherapy and radiation, which was a huge stretch for someone from a traditional upbringing. He did, however, accept surgery as a must, and I supported his decision. "I'll postpone surgery for two weeks," he declared, "if you will come down and work with me." I flew down with my new baby, and my father put himself in my care.

It seemed so natural to guide him through mind/body work, diet, affirmation and prayer. *He was taking back control of his life.* We worked intensely night and day for two long weeks. With support from our entire family, he realized his worth and how much he meant to us. He declared his right to live! He became so confident with the new wisdom that we could see his fear disappear. Like a closed blossom showing its face to the new light of the season, his health was renewing, and all possibilities were opening.

On the fifteenth day, he proceeded with his plan and admitted himself for surgery, maintaining confidence in his ability to heal. The whole family gathered in the waiting room. At last the surgeon came out. He was pleased to report that the tumor was no longer visible to the human eye! Ten years have gone by and my father is alive and well. There were so many "gifts" in that ugly package—renewed love and life, and further preparation for my soul's healing work with my patients.

YOUR STORY

I hope that when you listen to my stories, you will look at your own story and see things differently—with more hope. I picture you seeing your puzzle pieces—pretty or not—magically fitting together. If even one idea in this book can enhance your life, then I will know I am useful.

Come along with my courageous patients and me. Let's journey together, take by take, one realization at a time. As you open your new gifts in each chapter, may you see how your life lessons are preparing you for your higher greatness. You'll be astonished as you discover how many powerful gifts are waiting inside . . . YOU.

With an overflowing heart, I now pass these revelations on to you!

The Gift
of Taking

There I was, back in time,

listening to the wisdom

of the ages.

"Oh my goodness!" I whispered.

"We've got it all backwards—

*The gift is in the **taking**."*

Honor Myself First

Please, God, just give me back my life!
All I want is to be a great wife and mother
and to continue to help people along my journey.

As I prayed, a sense of peace came over me and the fear subsided. My higher self spoke: *Not only is he going to be all right, but you are going to help many others along the way.* I felt calm and drifted off to sleep.

It had been three long years, and I had given all that I had to give. My husband, Danny, had been diagnosed with a malignant brain tumor. So willingly, I had given up my practice and dedicated almost all of my time to helping him heal his life. We had worked endlessly, and our enduring efforts and devotion had at last paid off. We had succeeded! He was well on his way to a full recovery. Now it was I who was exhausted. I was missing my life as it had been before. I wanted to move past this. I cried out a prayer to God to help me.

TAKING BACK OUR LIVES

Within moments of my prayer, the phone rang. It was Danny. His words spilled out excitedly: "The most amazing thing happened, Jill! I was standing in the center of the circle at my men's group. It was my turn. Everyone was listening to me and I started my usual

Why me?, complaining about my life and the cards I had been dealt. Then suddenly, out of nowhere, I felt a sensation come over me. I turned to the men and said, *I am so tired of complaining . . .*

    All I want is my life back! I want to be a good husband and father and to help as many people as I can. I want my music back.

Danny and I had prayed for the exact same thing at the same time!

The next morning, Danny picked up his guitar for the first time in years. It looked so natural—as if it were part of his body. He walked, talked and slept with it all day, every day. He couldn't stop playing. It was so beautiful to have his music in our home again.

For many years, Danny had done all the "right" things. He was a successful chiropractor; he loved our wonderful children and me. We had a lovely home and a close community of friends. Yet something deep inside of him still felt unsettled. He felt guilty for feeling this way since on the outside it looked like he had it all. Nevertheless, something important was missing. For years he couldn't figure out where the emptiness was coming from. It took his illness to make him stop and sense his inner truth—that his passion was being a musician. When he honored that part of himself, his heart opened up and the healing came flowing in.

The same day Danny reunited with his music, a neighbor called and asked if I would help her with her back pain. Then another call came and another. For hours at a time, Danny played and played and played, rediscovering the music in his soul. He was elated to discover that his gift of music inspired and helped others as well. Within two weeks, my own practice was going strong again. I was getting calls from all over the United States from cancer patients, people with emotional problems, and people with other kinds of illnesses. The referrals seemed endless. Our prayers had been answered. We both got our lives back, in even better ways than we could have imagined. And all we had to do was ask. That experience was my first step in learning how to receive.

My practice grew even more, because, in addition to correcting the alignment of the spine, I was now helping people overcome the kind of thinking that contributes to illness and holds them back. It felt wonderful. My career was branching out. By 1998, my creative *interactive realizations* were inspiring patients to new levels of healing.

By this time, Danny was a full-time professional musician performing and writing inspirational songs that impacted people's lives. He had never felt so happy. Our young family had stabilized. I couldn't imagine why I was now beginning to feel restless myself.

TURNING THE TABLES: WHAT DO I WANT?

One night in 1999, Danny took me out to dinner. I launched into my caretaker mode. How did he want to proceed with his healing? How could I help? What did he want to do with his newfound music career? He stopped me and said, "Jill, I'm going to be just fine. Stop focusing on *me*. What do you want for *your* life?"

That stopped me in my tracks. I couldn't imagine how he could even ask such a question! What a concept! What do I want for *me?* The only satisfaction I had ever known was in caring for others, and I thought that was enough for me. Nevertheless, maybe concentrating only on others was where my restlessness was coming from. Danny asked, "If there were no limitations, and you could do anything in this world, what would that be?" *I didn't know.* Yet the seed was planted. He had given me a gift. I had thought I was content at my present level, but while I was definitely passionate about my work and family, in the back of my mind I started stretching, wondering.

Outside of the restaurant, I turned to Danny and, out of the blue, I said, "I want to be like Louise Hay!" It was a big pronouncement, and he looked at me in surprise. "You've never said anything like that before." Louise Hay is a world-renowned healer who healed her life when she had a terminal illness and now helps people from all over the globe to heal their own lives. We laughed as if it were a far-off dream, and we went home.

ANOTHER LIFE-CHANGING PRAYER

As the year progressed, I realized that my gift is the ability to open myself up and guide others through their emotional and spiritual voids. It seemed natural for me to guide people back into their lives. I watched them expand their realities and rise to higher levels. Using the techniques I taught them, they declared their right to a powerful, happy life and then proceeded with confidence in good health! I felt very grateful for this gift and always looked for more wisdom and guidance.

A year later, on a day in February 2000, something happened. I started to feel selfish. Not a bad type of selfish, but rather as if I were withholding something wonderful that I had to give.

Cascading through my mind all day were these thoughts:

Why keep this purely for my patients?
I wish more people could know about this!
Why help only one person at a time
if I could spread this message and help so many more?

For most of us, the fear of change is enormous, and it was for me on that day as well. I kept visualizing how so many people all over the world could benefit from this information! However, the thought of spreading this knowledge felt overwhelming. Change? Me? Should I? Well, this is what I teach! "Walk into your fear or resistance. Your lessons are on the other side." I shifted my thinking from

How could I possibly do this?

to

The timing is perfect. I'm ready!

It was no longer a question of *if* I should proceed, but *how*.

That night when I went to bed, I said my little prayer with trust and belief that I would be guided:

Dear God, if I am to be a catalyst to spread this word to our world,
I am ready to accept the responsibility.
Please help me, because I have no idea how to do this.

~

The very next morning, in between patients, my phone rang. It was Bonnie, a woman who had started out as a patient and turned into a friend. She attributes much of her emotional growth to our work together. Her words were going a mile a minute. "Jill, you'll never believe this!" Then she laughed and said, "On the other hand, knowing you, you will! I was asked to be the publisher for a national women's magazine. Will you write for me on health and healing each month?" I couldn't believe my ears! I had prayed for a way to spread the word only the night before, and here it was! Now I'd have a platform for sharing my messages. I was thrilled beyond belief.

Later that same day, I received another phone call. It was the director of the healing services at a local Unity Church. Several church members had reported that I had helped them. She asked if I would honor them and lead one of their healing services. My excitement exploded! Things were happening so fast! I thought, *O.K., Spirit, we're moving now!* I embraced the pace.

Then my patient Debbie arrived, and what started as a routine session unfolded into much more—something that changed both of our lives forever. Here's how it began:

The Birth of the Gift of Taking

LIGHTS, CAMERA, ACTION!

I was beginning to see the big picture. The lights turn on, the cameras roll—then ACTION! Our life script begins. As the reels turn, there we are on the big screen playing out our roles, one realization after another. Take after take, we try to get it right.

Debbie had been doing her best to get it right. She was ready to review her own life story. She couldn't understand why she wasn't getting the results she wanted when she seemed to be doing everything "right." She was struggling and not seeing her own value.

LOST IN THE MAZE OF GIVING: DEBBIE'S STORY

Debbie owned and operated a local herb store. She was extremely knowledgeable in her trade, and people consulted with her daily, gaining valuable information that she shared lovingly and openly. She was giving her heart and soul to help a woman who was interested in franchising a store like hers in another country. Debbie spent endless days with her, never thinking about compensation while educating and informing this woman about her business.

Debbie, like so many of us, was taught from an early age to think of others first. She gave, day after day—to the point of depletion. She was still awaiting her reward. Everything was a struggle. She was drained emotionally, physically and financially. She looked at me and said, "I just don't get it. There's something missing in this equation. I'm doing all the right things. I give and I give and I give. Why aren't I successful? Maybe I'm just not giving enough. If only I could give more, I would!"

Boy, did this sound familiar! She was a mirror image of myself last year. I was certainly in a position to understand her challenge. Reflecting on her thoughts, I guided her through the session, helping her balance her life.

Suddenly, something different happened. I felt a rush inside my head, and I heard words. An amazing insight was revealed. I blurted out to Debbie: "NO, NO, NO. It's not about the *giving*. It's all about the *taking*! TAKE, TAKE, TAKE!"

My eyes opened wide. I looked around and everything seemed so clear. A hidden consciousness had just been born. It felt like something planted long ago had just blossomed. My mind's doors opened wide and the truth came marching in. There I was, back in time, listening to the wisdom of the ages.

"*Oh my goodness,*" I whispered. "*We've got it all backwards!*"

Debbie looked at me, puzzled. "What in the world are you talking about?"

The voice and messages were coming through stronger and clearer now. I repeated, "We've got it all backwards. You can never *give* to another unless you have already *taken*! We must first learn to *take*, so we can replenish and honor ourselves."

Confused, Debbie asked, "What do you mean? Isn't taking selfish?"

I didn't answer her right away, because a question kept rolling around my head: *What's more important in life—to give or to take?* I presented it out loud. Debbie trusted me, yet couldn't imagine why I asked her such a simple question. "Of course," she immediately said, "to give!"

By now I was listening very deeply and was hearing: *The answers are all mirrored in nature. Think of the tree.* I asked Debbie, "Is the tree a giver or taker?" With no hesitation, she blurted out, "GIVER! Trees give us oxygen, shade, wood and fruit." The conviction of her answer was deeply imbedded within her mind.

To her surprise, I said, "No, trees are TAKERS!"

"No way!" she responded.

"Think about it," I encouraged. "The tree 'takes' what it needs— energy from the sun, nutrients from the soil, and water to replenish itself. Then to maintain its balance it overflows its surplus as the gift—oxygen—our breath of life!"

"Wow," said Debbie. "Why haven't we thought of this before?"

I went on. "Trees don't stop to ask, *I wonder if the people in Japan or the United States or India need more oxygen?* All they care about is *taking* to honor and replenish themselves, and we receive the over- flow of their abundance—the oxygen, the shade, the flowers, the fruit. We can take those gifts, use them to replenish ourselves, and in turn we'll have gifts to overflow to the world."

"No wonder we've all been feeling deprived," Debbie said.

I continued questioning Debbie, excited by the concept of *taking:* "Is the sun a giver or a taker?"

"I would have said giver for sure since it gives us sunlight. But I have the feeling you're going to challenge that . . ."

"You're right." I was staring straight into the center of the sun, watching how it utilized its life force. I replied, "Our sun is a powerful ball of energy that constantly takes from the energies of the universe. Its purpose in life is to replenish itself. It remains abundant from taking and honoring itself first, then it automatically overflows its excess rays. The by-product of its energy is our sunlight. That is its gift to our world—the sunshine upon our land."

By now Debbie was intrigued, and I couldn't stop. It was as if something had taken over, and revelations were moving so fast I could hardly keep up. "The sun listens to its inner voice. Its innate intelligence stays in alignment with the universe and Mother Nature, and it constantly *takes!* The overflow—its light—is a by-product to keep itself in balance."

"So the sun is a taker, too," said Debbie.

"Yes. The only way the sun is able to give light to the plants, nourish us with vitamins and warmth, and provide growth for all living beings is by honoring itself first. All of its gifts come to us *only* because it *takes* first. Only after it *takes* are we able to reap the benefits of its overflow."

"Wow," said Debbie. "It seems so simple. If we all were honoring ourselves first, we'd all be living in abundance—and sharing abundance!"

"Exactly. We'd stop waiting for someone else to fill us up!"

This revelation was amazing. When Debbie and I realized the gift we had been given and how powerful the message was, we knew that something very exciting had just overflowed to us. We stopped talking, thinking the same thing:

The gift is in the taking.

Maybe we have all been thinking backwards our whole lives. We were taught to be givers; we were raised to put everybody else first, and that it is selfish to take for ourselves. But maybe taking is *not* an act of selfishness. Maybe *taking* is an act of responsibility and inner direction.

OVERFLOWING

That morning of enlightenment moved something wonderful within me. I felt so alive! The revelation I had received seemed so pure and simple. To share abundance we must honor and replenish ourselves first. I knew I must now overflow and share this concept! Eagerly, I shared the revelation with all of my patients that day. I knew that this message could forever change peoples' lives for the better. My patients listened and absorbed like sponges, challenging their old thought patterns. Their spirits began to soar as new realizations came to life. They didn't want to leave, yet they couldn't wait to run and share this concept with their friends and family, overflowing to everyone they knew.

MORE REVEALED

That evening, everyone in the family was asleep except me. I was trying to drift off, but my thoughts kept waking me, each one triggering another. The feeling was amazing, as if something had taken over, yet it felt so right. I grabbed a stack of paper and started writing like crazy. My mind and my hand were on automatic pilot. The messages started coming faster and faster. If I didn't write them down, they would be gone forever. I was writing so furiously that I never even had time to look at or process any of it. I wrote all through the night.

PAGES OF MYSTERY

The next morning I read what I had written—pages and pages of revelations. I had written about our responsibilities to ourselves and agreements we made *before we even entered this world!* Where was this coming from? It was an overflow of all that I ever knew and more, yet presented so much better. It felt as if all my thoughts were being collected in such an amazing sequence and dispensed so remarkably. I pored over all the papers, trembling in awe. I knew I had connected to my true source, and I felt enormous gratitude.

I had received a supreme gift. As I read, I took every word to heart, with the pure intent of building upon my life's purpose and meaning so that I could share with my patients, family and friends.

After writing most of the night, I should have been exhausted, but I was exhilarated! It was 6 A.M. and I had a full day of patients scheduled to start in four hours. My adrenaline was flowing and I was energized beyond belief. My mind and soul were completely open. I couldn't contain the revelations any longer.

I glanced over at my husband, who was still sound asleep. Like a tornado, I scooped up the papers, shook him awake and kissed him. He blinked and woke up fast, dazed by my ecstasy. My words came spilling out so fast I could hardly say them. Completely awake now, Danny said, "Let me see." We sat in bed astonished, scanning the stacks of pages. We read . . .

LIFE IS A GRAND MYSTERY
You are made to succeed!

SOUL PURPOSE
From the moment of existence all life systems were set up for advancement. Like all miracles of nature, your soul has purpose and meaning. Your purpose is revealed in the unknown. Your soul enters this world for one reason. It's hungry! Its only intent is to learn and grow. Your job is to supply the food. The quality of food that nourishes your soul is directly proportional to the quality of your

thoughts. Yes, soul food is food for thought. You form your personality for the sole purpose of feeding your soul. In turn, this process determines the quality of your life.

SOUL FOOD

You replenish yourself and form your personality by the quality of your soul food—your choices, moment by moment. As you reveal your choices, you begin to uncover the mysteries of life. Within each moment of time, you gather information, interpret experiences around you, and form your perceptions, which make up who you are in that moment. When you are living and honoring the true intent of your soul, you always create closeness in your life. Using the unknown as your guide, you proceed, with a hunger for advancement. You seek knowledge by challenging yourself into a growth state. Your personality qualities are then called Self, and they become the gifts you have to share. Your gifts automatically overflow as a reflection of who you are and what you represent to the world, moment by moment.

THE BRAVEST SOULS

You are the bravest soul of all, a spiritual being daring to live in a physical world with a physical body; daring to explore and learn your lessons by conquering limitations, by working with and utilizing the only live energy that exists: THE MOMENT. All your lessons will come by over-coming the limitations that are presented to you. How you fill and cycle energy through your space determines the effectiveness of your lessons, and, in turn, creates your destiny.

You picked your part; you chose your role—to be a performer in the big picture of life. The part you con-tracted for lands you in the middle of the Grand

Mystery. By playing a part and being a part of the whole, you will expand, stretch and exercise your mind, body and soul to higher levels of knowingness.

THE HARDEST AND MOST GRATIFYING CHALLENGE

Within this way of life, you are set apart. It is the most difficult role to find your way through the unknown, yet it is also the most rewarding. In the physical world, there is much gratification. You are able to savor the sweet taste of the strawberry, thrill to the sight of the soaring eagle, succumb to the intoxicating scent of jasmine, be mesmerized by the rhapsodic tones of a string quartet. You are able to feel the sensations and emotions from embracing each other, crying, kissing the nape of a baby's neck, experiencing the ecstasy of uniting as one . . . There are so many gifts to experience in gratitude in this physical life, yet it is challenging at the same time.

EVERYTHING IS MYSTERIOUS

Within the physical plane, everything is mysterious! As you continue to move through your role in life, you never know the next clue until it is presented. It is a trust game—you never know what the next moment will bring. It becomes a multi-player show. You must figure out ways to transport yourself in and out of lessons utilizing support. When you take to replenish your soul, your life will create a magnetic force that attracts others who wish to support you and who will also benefit from your abundance. The quality of the replenishment taken will create closeness with others as it aligns with the true intention of your soul, creating a balance of space within self.

Taking, replenishing and building upon one live

*energy at a time, moment by moment, you create
momentum in your life—the only "live" active energy
for your performance. Within every moment you can
unfold an unknown. The mystery of why that lesson
occurred and how that piece fits into the whole will
enhance your growth process. Then the search for the
next clue continues. At times you will not know why a
piece of the mystery was presented. You must trust and
save it for later. Trust that it is always preparation for
an even bigger picture.*

At this point Danny and I were truly speechless. Danny, the song-writer, wrote down this formula:

Our Gift: *The Unknown*
Our Purpose: *To Take, to Learn and Succeed*
The Key to Success: *The Moment*
Our Method: *Trusting Our Choices in Each Moment*
Our Fate: *Soul Food Lessons Creating Destiny*

Before, we had always feared the unknown. Now it seemed we had *that* backwards, too! Trusting the unknown is where the power lies! It makes everything that is handed to us in life seem like a gift. Now we can be assured that even the most challenging difficulties are a gift in disguise! We read on.

*Before life there is life; after life there is life; you are
life! You are spiritual beings, belonging to a collective
awareness—a God-consciousness. Your spirit lives for all
eternity and your knowledge and wisdom always
remains within. As partners with God, you expand your
independent soul in alignment with God and the universe. This alliance creates the balance of the whole.*

As we were deep in concentration, reading about the balance of our entire universe, our alarm clock rang! We hated to be interrupted, but it was time to wake the kids for school. We jumped out of bed and zoomed around the house in record time. Once the kids were dressed, fed, and off to school, we landed back on the bed and hungrily continued reading:

SAFEKEEPING

The wisdom of your years and lifetimes are accumulated and stored within you, embracing your soul. Your supreme wisdom—also known as past experiences—is secured deep within. Your cumulative essence as a spiritual being is placed in safekeeping. In all other settings beyond this plane, you have access to and can use your highest knowingness from all your historical experiences. In lieu of building upon all the knowingness you have gathered within your spirit over all the lifetimes in the universe, you will set aside all past lessons and begin all over. You will grow your spirit without the use of your total wisdom of your existence.

CLEAN SLATE

On Earth, you start over at the time of conception. With a clean slate you learn and grow in some of the most difficult, most stimulating ways. Once you have fully expanded in this experience, you return to the universe and simultaneously reclaim all of your past awareness. Your adventure creates an expanded reality, adding dimension to your soul. Your preference to move on to another growth experience, or rest in the silence between, remains open. You now and forever remain in choice.

Talk about power! The two of us were reeling with the energy from these revelations. We marveled at the concept: *Taking is a reflection of feeding our soul.* When we can *take* and create closeness, we know we are honoring ourselves and helping others at the same time! So taking isn't selfishness. As we *take,* we challenge our thoughts into the next growth state and we expand as spiritual beings. As we stretch with joy and fulfillment, our whole world grows with us. This must be how we fulfill our purpose.

The energy in the room seemed infinite, and life seemed lighter. I looked at my watch and found that our moment together had turned into three hours! It was time for work. My husband, the man who had recently rediscovered his true self as a musician, said with a smile, "I feel a song coming on." We both knew it was going to be a great day. We couldn't wait to find out . . .

What's next?

The Gift
of Trusting

The answers are

all mirrored

in Mother Nature.

You are the eye

of the hurricane.

Do not get caught

in the winds.

My Inner Voice Is My Guide

IT'S MY TURN!

The endless energy of a child continued to blast through me. The feeling was amazing. My whole being was revved up from all the messages and insights I was receiving. I felt so cherished inside, I was like the little kid on the playground saying, *Now it's my turn!* Yes, I knew it was my turn. Like a child, I had asked for what I wanted, and the universe had sent it to me.

That morning felt like a holiday. Every realization was like opening up another present. I couldn't wait to see what gift would be revealed in the next moment! Even though it was almost time for my first patient to arrive, I *had* to read what came next on the mysterious pages I had written.

> *You have contracted an agreement as my partner. I have embedded lasting impressions within your mind, soul, and body as constant reminders of your responsibilities to who you are and what you represent to our world.*

Lasting impressions? Responsibilities? Constant reminders? I was so curious; I wanted to know more. I was eager to greet my patients and share all of the magnificent gifts that had been revealed. I just knew that once they saw how we are doing it all backwards, an amazing enlightenment would come over them and they'd get it!

Donna, my first patient, drove up, and I bubbled over with excitement, anticipating the impact my revelations would have on her. I just knew that the incredible words from the night before would inspire her. I could see the whole picture: she walks through the door, I share these realizations, she immediately claims her power and declares her right to live in abundance and share from abundance. I envisioned the two of us like kids on the playground—running from realization to realization, feeling the thrill of the moment. My energy would trigger hers, and hers would trigger mine into more insights. When we parted, I would continue to enlighten my patients throughout the day, and they would run out the door to enlighten everyone in their world. It just seemed so clear!

I DON'T KNOW WHO I AM ANYMORE

Donna walked through the door. Her head was down. She looked at me with tears flowing and said, "There must be more to life than this." Talk about slowing down! My energy went from two thousand miles per hour to zero in a millisecond. I took a deep breath, centered myself and listened. She lamented, "There's never enough time in the day. There's never enough money. All I do is take care of the kids, clean the house and pay bills. What about *me?* I'm always tired. I can't get enough rest. My husband and I never get quality time anymore. My whole life is going by and I'm just going through the motions. I don't even know who I am anymore!"

Donna knew that some of my work involved helping people balance mind, soul and body. She asked, "Do you do energy work?

Because that's just what I need—energy. I'm so tired of being drained and feeling overwhelmed!"

She was standing in my office, sad and depressed, reaching out for help. She felt detached from who she once was and what she had wanted for her life, and it was all very confusing to her. *How can you feel so empty,* she thought, *when you love your children, adore your husband and have a great life?*

Something was still missing and she couldn't figure it out. She just knew she wasn't fulfilled. How is an intelligent, loving person who was once on her path in life swayed off so innocently?

Loyal to a Fault: Donna's Story

Donna met her love in business school. They married shortly after they graduated. She dreamed of climbing the corporate ladder. "I couldn't wait to go out into the world and prove myself and make my dreams come true! I would have a great husband, a great job, and someday we would start a family. Shortly after graduation, I found out I was pregnant. That was a surprise. I hadn't planned on a baby so soon. But I was happy to have a son and I would make it work. I'd be both a mother and a businesswoman!

"I tried working and keeping my little one in daycare, but every day I felt so torn. When I was at work, I felt guilty, so I turned down promotions that would take time away from my family . . ."

"And each time you did that, your own dream was crumbling away."

"Yes. I was so stressed out. That's when my mother offered to take care of my son in her home. Mom never approved of day-care. She said it would work out just fine. She would love and provide for him and take care of everything. It seemed so perfect at the time!

"Until she started making quiet comments like, 'Children really need their mothers,' or 'Children are only young once, and you're missing the best years.' She'd say, 'You can always have time to work, but you can't replace Mommy or the time you missed hearing him say Mama or Dada for the first time.' I was going crazy with guilt!"

"Your mother came from the traditional family thinking where Moms stay home with the kids and Dads work all their life to support their families—the way she was raised, with her mother right by her side."

"Yes," she agreed

"You were bombarded with silent messages from your Mom that left lasting impressions within you. Every day when you went to pick up your son, you heard reminders of your wrong choices." Donna's eyes opened with that thought. "You're right."

"Your mother was well-meaning. But those were *her* opinions, not yours. Right?"

"I guess so. Then it happened again. I became pregnant. I wanted to be loving and do the right thing, so I quit my job to stay home with my kids."

"The power of your mother's thoughts and beliefs actually started to feel like your own. I call this *being loyal to a fault*. We came into this world pure—whole and complete . . ." The messages from the night before were coming into in my mind.

"Donna, we are all born with this *huge* inner voice that always knows exactly what is right for us. This voice leads us from the moment we are conceived, forms us into the powerful person we call self, and creates the person we are today. This inner voice is so powerful that even without words it speaks very loudly."

GOD'S FIRST LASTING IMPRESSION

"The first lesson we learned when we entered this world was that life is here to support us. We trusted. Even from conception, our support system was developing in our mother's womb—the umbilical cord. We took all that we needed to replenish and provide for ourselves first! We created natural growth and balanced within. This system was created naturally to meet our needs."

We both got excited as these thoughts unfolded. Suddenly, another mystery was revealed. *"Our belly button!"* I exclaimed. "Our navel. That is a lasting impression to remind us of our responsibility to take what we need! To remind us that we can trust."

I was back up to two thousand miles per hour. "When our cord was cut, we were left with a lasting impression—our navel—to remind us that we were here to be supported. If we ever forget that, we can just look and we'll remember!" Donna smiled.

"After our cord was severed, our means of support changed, so *we* changed. We immediately adapted to our new surroundings and we trained people to take care of us. Even as brand new babies, we relentlessly used our voices to get what we needed. We trained our parents before we even learned to speak. When our inner voice said we were hungry, we cried, and Mom picked us up and held us. If that wasn't what we wanted, we cried again and she fed us.

"This process of teaching went on continuously, sometimes all through the night, until our needs were met. Our parents learned early on about our different ways of asking and they adapted and aligned. Knowing our own value, we never stopped crying out for what we needed. Our inner voice told us what was right and important for us at that time in our lives.

"Our sense of 'I' was formed immediately. 'I' meaning, 'I' know who I *am* and 'I' know what is right for me. When we were children, our respect for our responsibility to grow and learn always led us. No matter what challenges lay ahead, we rose to the next level of personal achievement. We were completely inner-directed. We always honored the timing of our process. When it was time to learn to roll over, we challenged ourselves to do it. Do you remember how your babies tried and cried, never giving up 'til they figured out how to roll over? And once we accomplished one task, we automatically advanced ourselves to the next step—sitting up.

"As we grew, we stayed strong to our conviction of self, and through our own eyes there was no question we could do, be and have it all. There was basically nothing anyone could do or say that could make us feel otherwise. We respected our inner trust to the highest degree. As we continued to listen so deeply from within, the direction of our life unfolded. Nothing could stop us now! By challenging our growth through our limitations, we developed and learned. As we stretched, we only rested long enough to gather ourselves up for the next step. One step at time we would fall, get up and try again and again."

"Yeah, you're right," Donna agreed. "I remember the feeling— the challenge of learning something as simple as tying my shoes all by myself. I was so proud!"

"We challenged ourselves into another learning process. As our minds learned, we started to understand the system. We were onto a new evolution of our soul. Think about this. Ask any child in the world, 'Whose turn is it?' and every one of them will say '*Mine! It's my turn!*' Through the eyes of a child, life is a great big gift and it's theirs to open and enjoy!"

Donna asked, "So why don't we adults enjoy it anymore? When did we lose that?"

"The human language was introduced," I said. "We started learning words like NO. We started hearing *Don't do this* and *Don't do that, That's good* or *That's bad,* and our conditioning began. We slowly started to listen to voices other than our own. We listened to the voices of our parents. Doubt started to set in slowly as our inner voice was challenged, and we began looking for approval from others. We wanted to please; to get it right. Then one day, before we knew it, it happened—we got lost from home! Our *own* home, our own *inner knowingness.* You already know how that works."

Donna nodded.

"After our parents, it's the voices of our peers. You remember how it goes. Something like this."

```
          INT. ICE CREAM PARLOR - DAY
An EIGHT-YEAR-OLD bursts joyfully into the shop
with a group of FRIENDS. They all gather around,
overwhelmed, and point to all the colorful pos-
sibilities behind the glass, pondering.

               YOUNG SALESGIRL
          So what do you want?

               EIGHT-YEAR-OLD
               (loud and proud)
          A great big vanilla cone!

                    FRIEND
               (mocking)
          Check that out. The baby wants
          vanilla.

LOUD DEROGATORY LAUGHTER. The eight-year-old
visibly shrinks.

                    FRIEND
          I'LL have the double dutch
          chocolate raspberry swirl in a
          waffle cone.

               EIGHT-YEAR-OLD
               (small voice)
          Oh, I mean, I'll have that,
          too.
```

Selling Out

"Right then and there," I continued, "We stopped listening from the inside and started listening to the outside. We started thinking *Maybe someone else knows something better than we do.* And as we grew up, we did it over and over again. Only now we're not talking about insignificant choices like ice cream flavors—we're doubting *all* of our choices.

"Like a child who is continually ignored, our inner voice got quiet; it went away. Then suddenly, without even realizing it, we were lost. We couldn't find our way home to that knowingness we once had. That's when we began the endless journey of looking for the answers from the outside. At that point we lost the vision of

'WHO AM I?'
and
'WHAT DO I REPRESENT TO THIS WORLD?'

"We are then outer-directed, and we spend our whole life looking for the wisdom to get right back to where we started! Ninety percent of the people on our planet never obtain the lives they really want. Many struggle with inner truths and learned patterns. We have become loyal to the familiar lessons that were forced upon us. Fearful of changing, we stay loyal to a fault. *What if I make the wrong decision? What if I fail?* Our minds have been carefully molded into a belief system. Is it really our voice? Maybe it's other peoples' programs playing inside our minds, dictating our lives.

"Our family and teachers have been taught by their family and teachers, who may have had different lessons and ways of learning than we do. It's an endless generational cycle of hand-me-down lessons. When we start believing the voices of others as truth instead of making choices that nurture our own souls, then we become outer-directed, sold-out—or as I express it, 'SOUL'D OUT.'

"Isn't it the same when a movie is sold out? It means you can't get in. The same holds true for our soul. When our soul is SOLD OUT we become outer-directed, and it's extremely difficult to get in again and hear the real show—*our* show! This cycle of listening outside of ourselves will go on for eternity until we take control, break the cycle, and take back our freedom—our own choice."

You could almost see the wheels turning in her mind as Donna tried to grasp this concept, but it was too close to home and too soon for her to fully understand it.

Your parents' teachings leave you with one kind of *lasting impression*—a silent message embedded in your mind as you learn behaviors. Sometimes these silent messages are placed inside us so subtly that we think *they're* really who we are. They come from our perceptions and from our experiences as we learn from others.

The second kind of lasting impression is the kind that God places within our mind, soul and body to remind us of who we *really* are.

Here is an example of the first kind of lasting impression—a learned silent message that left a lasting impression. I described a typical scenario outside of her life, showing her how we are programmed into believing that our parents' hopes, dreams, fears, worries and desires are our own.

THE ORIGINAL LEARNED SCRIPT

SILENT MESSAGES
THAT LEAVE LASTING IMPRESSIONS

CHILD, 7 YEARS OLD
I'm going to be a baseball
player when I grow up, or maybe an
astronaut or the president of the
United States. Wow, I can be anything! I am great!

MOM
Yes you are. You can be anything or
do anything. You are the greatest!

DAD
We're already proud of you, son.

CHILD, 10 YEARS OLD
I'm definitely going to be a baseball
player when I grow up. Maybe I'll be
on the Yankees or Mets. What do you
think, Dad?

DAD
You just might, son. But you
know, only a few make it to the
Majors . . .
        (Silent message: Maybe I won't be
        good enough)

CHILD
        (despondent)
Oh. Really?
        (Lasting Impression: Doubt sets
        in)

TEEN, 15 YEARS OLD
Mom, Dad, guess what? I made the var-
sity baseball team!

MOM AND DAD
        (unison)
That's wonderful!

                    TEEN
        Maybe I'll have a shot at the
        Mets after all! Do you think?
                (Looking for confirmation and
                approval)

                    MOM
        Why not? But you're also very
        good in science. Maybe you could get
        a teaching degree just in case...

                    DAD
        And you know you're always welcome to
        come into business with me, son.
                (Silent message: Better safe than
                sorry. Maybe they know what's
                best for me. Lasting impression:
                Don't take risks.)

INT. FATHER'S PLACE OF BUSINESS - DAY
The now 25-year-old son works to please his
father, but is listless.

                SON, 25 YEARS OLD
        Dad, I keep feeling inside that
        there's something else out there for
        me . . .

                    DAD
        C'mon on now. You can be very proud
        of the work you're doing here. You're
        making a good living, son.
                (Silent message: Settle)

INT. FATHER'S PLACE OF BUSINESS -
15 YEARS LATER - EVENING
Father and now 40-year-old son argue loudly.
Mother and the son's WIFE and young son come out
of the back room, alarmed.

                SON, 40 YEARS OLD
        I've had it! I'm outta' here!

He storms toward the door. His wife grabs
desperately for him, but he jerks away.

                            DAD
        He's just going through a mid-life
        crisis.
                (Silent message: Who am I?
                Nothing's working! I can't remem-
                ber what makes me happy anymore.
                I've got to follow my dreams . . .)

The middle-aged son hops in his new red Corvette
and roars away to pick up his 25-year-old blonde
girlfriend.

                            MOM
        He's out of his mind!
                (Silent message:Where did I go
                wrong?)

Ext. SAME PLACE OF BUSINESS -
25 YEARS LATER - DAY
Very elderly mother hobbles along with her son,
now 65. They look up at the sign bearing his
father's name.

                            MOM
        You'd better retire before you
        have a heart attack like your
        father.
                (Silent message: You can't handle
                it)

                    SON, 65 YEARS OLD
        Retire? But I'm not done yet.
        But maybe you're right . . . maybe it's
        time to leave it to the young 'uns.
                (Silent message: Mother always
                knew best. Anyhow, it's too late
                for me.)

INT. PLACE OF BUSINESS - DAY
65-year-old son is now training his 25-year-old
son to run the family business.

                            MOM
        There's a nice room with a view in my
        Miami Beach retirement home, son.

                (Silent message: Give up, follow
                the masses.)

```
                      SON
        Maybe I'll look into it.
             (Just do what's expected)

   INT. MIAMI RETIREMENT HOME
   80-year-old son sits alone, depressed, playing
   solitaire. Stares out the window at a baseball
   field where some young children are playing
   ball.

                 SON, 80 YEARS OLD
        I should have been a ball player.
```

Donna got it. "Whew. But I don't think our parents mean for it to be that way any more than we do."

"Of course not," I agreed wholeheartedly. "Parents almost always have the highest and best interest for us. Their intentions are well-meaning. When they were planning our birth, they didn't say, 'Let's have a child so we can mess her up.' They were delighted to share and guide us the best way they knew. They believed that passing down these traditional family ways was the right thing to do. Because they were sure their way was the 'right' way, they led us, one thought at a time, and we followed. Maybe those thoughts worked for them in their lives, but they might not be right for us in ours.

"Now we must make a choice," I declared. "Which impressions do we want to be the *lasting* ones? Those of *others*, like our parents? Or our *own*—which are divinely inspired?"

You could almost see a light turn on over Donna's head. This one shift in her thinking had given her hope. Now there was a plausible reason for the void she felt inside; a reason she felt drained. It was making sense. She was living someone else's dream—her mom's! Now she understood why her picture-perfect life seemed so out of focus. She wasn't using her *own* purpose and gifts in balance with her family life.

I redirected her thoughts. "Tell me again about you and your career. What did you want? How did you see yourself?" She began slowly, trying to recall those past dreams. Then, as she remembered, her voice became stronger and her face lit up.

DONNA'S REALIZATION

"I was so full of hopes and dreams. I knew I was good at what I did. I excelled quickly. I was going to be the best darned corporate executive you ever saw!

"That dream was such a part of me—it was how I saw myself. But somehow it got lost. I thought I could do both: have my career and take care of my family. That idea came from a higher place of thinking. But then I let guilt and my mother's opinion erode my conviction. I went to the opposite extreme and gave up on myself—my career dreams—completely."

She suddenly glowed with knowingness. She had just heard for the first time that a balanced life requires using our gifts to fulfill our purpose and bring meaning to our life. That insight landed straight in the center of her heart, which opened. She said with resonating conviction, "I can work and use my talents to make my contribution and keep a balanced home at the same time! I'll be happier! So my family will benefit, too."

She had made the first step in trusting herself—giving herself permission. It was to be a process. I could help her see which inner childhood programming was useful and which silent lasting impressions needed to be discarded. I could give her the tools for releasing the memories that no longer served her. And I could give her new tools for making new choices.

Now I could see that God's plan revealed to me the night before was even more powerful than I had imagined. We can never give someone an outcome without allowing them to go through their own healing process. The gift of taking is in the lessons and in our choices.

Donna looked straight at me, and her eyes were filled with tears once more, but this time they were tears of joy, for she made a choice. "I'm ready," she said. She was ready to be guided into taking responsibility for her life—to find her inner voice and start listening and trusting from the inside once again. I could see her eyes light up and I knew she was on her way home again.

THE VISION OF THE VOIDS

That night the wind blew ominously, and rain slashed against the windows. Everything seemed very three-dimensional to me. My thoughts were swirling: reflections of my childhood, thoughts of Donna's dilemma, memories of the incredible insights from the night before. Once again, to my dismay, I could not fall asleep. I felt as if I were in another world. I wondered, with trepidation, what was going to happen next. As I stared out my window I could hear a message repeated steadily.

The answers are all in nature.

I heard it over and over again. *Mirror Mother Nature.* I saw a vision of a hurricane. Something started to happen. I started to feel as if I were spinning. *Stay centered,* I kept thinking. I then heard,

> *Do not get caught in the winds. You are the eye of the hurricane. The answers are all there. Allow the winds to carry you in and out of this experience. Always remember that you are the silence within the storm. Keep your focus on the eye, the rest will follow . . .*

I trusted very deeply as I drifted off into my childhood. There I was, listening to Mom and Dad playing out the old scenarios. There was so much screaming! It was so loud! *Stay in the center of the storm. Your answers are all there,* I heard. I sensed my soul moving. It felt as if it were being pulled apart. Openings were being created, as if someone were digging a hole right in the center of my soul.

"I don't understand! Help!" I cried. I could see myself reaching in as if a wound had been created. I just wanted to comfort the space. The tears started to flow. Then suddenly the spaces started to fill. My life's lessons were being poured into the openings and my soul began to expand. It was astounding. As the energy began to slow down, a realization appeared:

> *My childhood experiences were my gifts. All of them,*
> *good and bad. They were the winds that helped carry me*
> *in and out of my life's experiences. Our voids, our holes,*
> *are the Holy Spaces that God gave us. Through the*
> *winds of our past, the fertile soil of our soul is tilled,*
> *prepared so we can use our greatness and reach deep*
> *within ourselves to fulfill our life's work. As we grow*
> *and expand, our spirit follows.*

These impressions of holy spaces were now imbedded in my mind and soul.

Before, I had acknowledged these feelings as pain; but now the painful voids felt like sacred spaces. My childhood experiences became my blessings. I understood that voids are created within our lives so that these holy spaces can be prepared to fill with our life's work. We are the leaders of our own life. We choose the direction of our winds.

Choosing a New Direction for Myself

The rest of the night I was tired, yet charged at the same time. I just sat in bed, leaning on a pillow, wishing I could fall asleep. My room was dark. I found myself staring at the keypad of my house alarm—an ordinary panel of ivory-colored buttons. I could feel something almost moving in the room, even though I knew everyone else in the house was asleep. I could not take my eyes off that alarm pad. I was riveted to it. Suddenly, something appeared superimposed on the buttons that looked the dark gray shadow of a cross. I kept looking at it, wondering if I were imagining the shadow because I was so tired. I closed my eyes, shook my head and looked away, but my curiosity took over. I looked at the keypad again. The shadow of the cross was still there. "What is this?" I wondered. "Is this real?" So I asked Spirit, "O.K., what are you trying to tell me? I know you're here, I know you're trying to say something. But I just can't hear you."

As I continued to stare at the keypad, my mind started to drift. Maybe the cross was a sign. I closed my eyes and turned my head sideways to see if it were still there. It was—clear as day, right on the keypad, a great big cross. All night long I kept wondering and asking. I never understood the message that night.

The next day was Saturday. I called my parents to share my amazing experience of the past two days. I sensed my dad listening intensely. When I came to the part about my realization of *taking*, he went wild!

"This is the most incredible insight I've ever heard, Jill!" he said. "You are so right. We are all giving our lives away, depriving ourselves. We are waiting and putting off *our* right to success, thinking we are taking away from somebody else's! It reminds me of flying on an airplane when the stewardess explains, *In case of an emergency, take care of your self first.*"

We talked for an hour, thinking of every possibility that comes from taking. Then he stopped and said, "This is too incredible. Write a book, Jill, write a book! People *must* hear this!"

The idea of a book was overwhelming. I'm a great healing doctor, but not truly a writer. However, the more he talked about it, the more I realized he was right. This is such a powerful message. A book would be a great way for others to learn about it. I said, "You're right. I'll write a book!"

He immediately asked, "O.K., what are you going to call it?"

Without hesitation I blurted out, *"The Gift of Taking."*

"Incredible!" he said. "What's the cover going to look like?"

Immediately I saw it. "A shiny white cover wrapped like a present, with a red ribbon and a big red bow. And a gift card on the cover: *From: Dr. Jill.* This will be my gift to our world."

I was so excited. After I hung up, I ran downstairs. I wanted to draw the cover before I forgot it. I picked up a piece of white paper and grabbed a pencil. I drew the ribbon. Two lines down, then two lines across. As I stared at this drawing, all I could see was my alarm pad. *And the cross.* My tears started flowing and I looked up at the heavens and said, "Thank you, God, that's what you were trying to tell me all night long. You were giving me the cover of my book, before I even knew I was to write a book! I am in awe of this process!"

I had opened the gift of *trusting.* I was beginning to realize that we are in partnership with God. I felt so inspired, but there was still much to wonder about, opening up a new floodgate of questions. *How does it all work? Who does what? What are the responsibilities of my patients? What are my responsibilities in the contract?*

That was what I had to find out.

The Gift
of Wellness

For all eternity

there has been balance

in our universe.

As I created all sickness

and disease,

I simultaneously secured

all the answers.

The solutions now

and forever

remain within.

I Can Heal Myself

Ideas! Gifts! Possibilities! Amazing connections to my higher source! Realizations revealing secrets! Mysteries of life! Writing a book! I was in a state bordering on ecstasy. My soul was inspired to take these new realities, like an ever-expanding present, and overflow them to help others. This cycle of contribution was endless and was meant to be shared! I stood, as still as could be, with the opportunity I had requested before me—helping people on a higher level. I was receiving everything I had ever asked for. Suddenly, fear washed over me in equal proportion to the ecstasy.

DOUBT SETS IN

The grander dream moved me out of my comfort zone. I felt uneasy. How could *I* possibly write a book? To me, my gifts were obvious: I guided patients back to their optimum health on a one-on-one basis. I had never thought of myself as a writer, yet here I was, walking into a foreign land, and I didn't even speak the language.

Fear began to take hold. I wanted to retreat. The thought of undertaking such a monumental project now seemed tremendously scary. Would it even be possible to complete such a time-consuming project with my current workload and obligations? All of a sudden, as if my life were in reverse, I was like my patients—feeling fear as I came face-to-face with change. Was *I* willing to do what I ask of *them?* Could *I* walk into the resistance? I felt very vulnerable.

The phone interrupted my train of fear-producing thoughts. It was my friend Jay, eager to tell me a story. I didn't have time. I had important decisions to make. But a little voice inside reminded me to trust the timing of the universe.

He just heard about lion prides and how they hunt to get what they need. He explained that in the animal kingdom, the lions work instinctively to hunt their prey. The young lions in the pride are extremely fast and strong, yet their roar is weak because their vocal cords haven't developed fully. The older lions aren't as fast or strong, but have the loudest, most impressive roars in the kingdom.

Instinctively, the two generations of lions set themselves up for success by separating and working together on a kill. When their prey comes close, the younger lions and older lions stalk on opposite sides. The older lions move in behind and roar fiercely. Terrified, the prey runs away from the loud roar straight into the jaws of the swifter young lions!

RUN TOWARD THE ROAR!

I said, "That's a wonderful story! But what does it mean?"

"Jill, don't you get it?" Jay said. "The moral of the story is: *Always run toward the roar, for that is where your safety lies!*"

I hung up the phone with the story echoing in my head. *Mirror Mother Nature.* That message again. The book idea was roaring at me and scaring me away from it. Of course! *Run toward the roar. Toward* the book, not away from it. That was exactly what I needed to hear. I knew that all this valuable inspiration I'd been receiving would disappear and be lost forever if I did not act immediately. Jay's story was not an interruption after all, but help at the exact moment I needed it.

I was beginning to see that all this incredible information was only as good as the action I was willing take to share it. I had to coach myself now; asking only the questions that I knew would give me confidence. How would it make me feel if I captured this knowledge into a book form?

I knew it would bring me a huge sense of accomplishment. I could help even more people reclaim their health. I could envision their most precious commodity—themselves—being restored. Putting the focus on the goal and the results made my fear fade into the background. My original impulse to overflow and contribute became even stronger.

Now, seeing the fear as my *savior,* I began to work on my solution. I made a switch. Just as I coached my patients into solution-oriented thinking, I did the same for myself. I got right into the action—the work to be done. As my mind raced ahead, it felt like the storm had blown through. A calm came over me. I was hearing and thinking on a deeper level once more:

> *Remember to come from abundance, not fear or deprivation.*
> *The book is only the beginning. When it is complete,*
> *put your visualizations on tape.*
> *People all over the world will be able take responsibility*
> *for healing their lives without your presence.*
> *Spread this information to the world.*

At first I was stunned. This assignment would add even more responsibility to my project. The roar was getting louder! It was a challenge to run toward it. But I was ready. I had never been great at asking for things on my own behalf, but I certainly was getting the hang of it. When spirit talked, I listened! I just never imagined how *fast* my prayers would be answered. I marveled and was grateful. I was open to expanding my story once again.

MORE UNVEILED MYSTERIES

But how? How would I start to write this book? With no guidelines or knowledge to help me, I went back to my power of trust. I scanned through my notes, trying to organize my thoughts, and this prompted more and more thoughts. I began writing at a rapid pace, and by the next morning, I had a stack of new information, but I decided to set it all aside. The idea of stimulating more insights was overwhelming. I had already been up for three straight days, writing frenetically, treating patients, and caring for my family. I needed rest.

Sunday was supposed to be a relaxing day. I looked forward to unwinding and turning off my mind. The kids were joyfully running in and out of the house with their friends; Danny was relaxing on the couch watching basketball on TV. I was simply happy doing absolutely nothing. But within moments, the peace was interrupted by the jangle of the phone. I sighed and picked it up. It was Sue, my wonderful mother-in-law. I could sense the panic in her voice and I shivered.

"What's the matter, Mom?" I asked.

THE BIG "C"

"Jill, I was just diagnosed with the Big "C" in the Big "B"—breast cancer."

My first thought was, *God, please, haven't we had enough cancer in one family?* My adrenaline started flowing. "How could this be? Are you sure?"

"Yes. I had a biopsy and it was confirmed."

I took a deep breath and she told me the whole story. As she spoke, I was getting flashbacks to her reaction when Danny was diagnosed with brain cancer. She had been so concerned for him, flying into town to be with her youngest son. Throughout the week she was here, she had said to him repeatedly, "If I could take this from you, I would." And she meant it!

I reminded her of that story and told her she didn't have to take it so literally! With her strong sense of humor still intact, she laughed. I told her she had better get well, because she is a staple in our family and we all love her.

After she hung up the phone, I couldn't stop thinking, *Why so many lessons through sickness and disease?* All day I felt as if there were a cloud over me. My mind was so preoccupied with the thought of cancer. I thought about my father's cancer, Danny's cancer, and my own cancer patients. Now cancer had once again struck my family, and I was disturbed.

There must be something we are not seeing, I kept thinking to myself.

My mind traveled all day, deeper and deeper into questions. By nightfall, I was exhausted. Before I fell asleep, I asked for guidance.

> *Please allow me more information to help my mother-in-law—*
> *and all cancer patients—heal themselves.*
> *Help me, God, so I can help others.*

I said the prayer over and over again.

DREAM SOLUTIONS

With this prayer heavily on my mind, I could hardly keep my eyes open and began drifting into a dream state. I dreamt that I was lying in a splendid green meadow staring straight up into a beautiful blue sky. Then, almost like magic, a word appeared in the formation of the clouds. It spelled out . . .

CANCER

I was captivated, staring at the word. Then the letter R began flashing. I couldn't lift my eyes from it. As I lay there staring at the letter R, these thoughts were roaming through my mind:

So many people with cancer are *resistant* to change, living in *resentment*, harboring *rage*, unwilling to take *responsibility*, feeling *remorse* and having *regrets*, being *rejected*.

It occurred to me that all of these words began with the letter *R*. As the words continued to cascade through my mind, my heart started beating fast. My mind kept flashing back to my patients and the stories of their lives. Their beliefs seemed to have led them to the school of cancer. Then I focused on how they learned so much and rose above cancer and healed their lives. My thoughts stirred passionately:

If everyone would just open up and start *listening*, then they would be *learning*. They would achieve their *lessons* and be in *life*, with *love* and *laughter*.

All I could think of were *L* words! I wanted so much for the world to share in these lessons that I reached into the sky, pulled down the flashing letter *R*, and replaced it with the letter *L*. And right before my eyes, the word CANCER changed to

CANCEL

I leapt out of bed faster then you can imagine and started writing again. Another secret revealed! *To cancel cancer and other illnesses, one must make take responsibility to shift from the Rs to the Ls.* As Spirit kept guiding me, I heard that we could do it by making the powerful *"C" connection.* The *C* was the Cure. *C* was being used to communicate back to self again. For a *connection,* one must be open to *change,* take *control* of life, and always stay in *choice*. All these C actions would contribute to bringing emotional balance back into our lives.

Curing the Big "C"

All night, revelations about how to heal cancer came faster than I could believe possible. I stayed open and wide awake. The following morning, how fitting it was that Carmen was my first patient of the day. Carmen had been seeing me for about two years and she had taken responsibility for her life. At age fifty, she had cured herself of Stage 4 breast cancer, which the doctors had deemed incurable.

Smiling and energetic, Carmen marched through my door. Here was a woman who had learned how to own both her power and all the rights to her life. I told her that I had had the most incredible dream about curing cancer. As you can imagine, she was thrilled. As I shared the past night's experience, I could feel her excitement building. She couldn't sit still. She was absorbing every word. Her eyes lit up as I related my realizations and experiences over the last four days. When I mentioned the idea of writing a book, she jumped right out of her seat and declared, "Please put my story in your book! I want my story to help as many people as possible. I want them to hear about how hopeless I felt and how you helped me turn that feeling around. I want them to experience believing in their true capabilities and in the possibilities that are out there for all of us."

Connecting to Health: Carmen's Story

"As I was developing in my mother's womb, my mother was retreating. Just as I entered this world, Mom checked out with breast cancer. What was to be the biggest celebration of my life—my birth—turned into total abandonment, sadness and mourning. I was surrounded by tears, pain, anger and confusion. I wonder now if maybe intuitively I felt that I would follow in my mother's footsteps. Deep down inside of me there was always a void.

"As I grew, I always attracted the wrong men. I'd fall head over heels in love, trying to *be* loved and to please, but it always ended up the same—the men would leave me. Later in life, I married and my life took a turn for the worse. Our marriage was stressful. Not content in his own life, I figured out later, my husband tried to make himself feel strong by tearing me down. My sense of self-worth diminished year by year.

"I gave birth to a beautiful baby girl, with the hope that things would get better. Instead, they got worse. I was so highly committed to making my marriage work that I stayed in it, and stayed miserable, for twenty-four years. I built up anger and resentment. I blamed myself, him and the whole world for my unhappiness. I just couldn't find the way out of this mess I had created. If I stayed, I'd sacrifice my happiness. But to me, leaving was bailing out. There were no answers.

"At night, I'd dream of a happy life, of finding love and fulfillment. But how could I leave? One day, I hit the point of no return. The resentment in my heart was so strong, and I knew I could not save or change my husband. The person who really needed saving was me. I had to leave. Yes, I declared my right to be happy—or at least my right to make a change. I filed for divorce. Little did I know how far from home I really was. I was 'free,' but I was still not in a good place.

"Then it happened. An unknown 'host' entered a room in my 'house' and the walls started crashing down. I was being divorced once again, only this time from my own body. The doctor told me the diagnosis: incurable breast cancer. The exact cancer that killed my mother. All the doctors agreed: 'We have no cure for your type of cancer. It is fatal. Surgery on a tumor this size is impossible. All we can do is chemotherapy to try to shrink it down a little, and see where we can go from there.'

"Once again, I felt stuck—damned if I did and damned if I didn't. The feeling was so familiar. Making my decision from a place of fear, I started the treatment. I weakened daily. I lost my hair, my resistance plummeted, my blood became infected, I had open lesions in my mouth from the chemotherapy. I couldn't eat, drink or swallow. I felt hopeless, yet still I continued this painful process. Deep down, I felt that my mother had passed this illness down to me. I was guilt-ridden that I would pass it on to the next generation—to my own daughter.

"For my daughter's sake, I tried to make it look as though I would be all right, but I knew that I wasn't. That's when my little angel Beth appeared. I hardly knew her. She was a friend of a friend who had been seeing Dr. Jill for a back problem.

"'When I found out about your situation, I wanted to help you in some way,' Beth said. 'I didn't feel that flowers or a warm meal would help out you as much as this.' She handed me a card. 'The best gift I can offer you is the phone number of my doctor. She works with cancer patients and I have a feeling you should call her.'

"I stared at the card for a while and then put it in my pocket and went home. *Could this be?* I thought. *Is it possible that someone out there could give me an answer other than 'It's hopeless'?* I took a deep breath, and something inside told me to call. I thank God daily for that call. That's when my life began again."

HEALING POWER

By the time Carmen reached me, her life had gotten so far out of balance that she was more than ready to listen. After she told me her story, I looked deep into her eyes and said, "All sickness and disease is curable. If anyone in this world has ever healed themselves from breast cancer—and I know of such cases—you can, too."

Her eyes lit up. She wanted so much to believe my words. I went on. "There's more than one way to get to a place. If you are going down one path and not finding it, that doesn't mean it doesn't exist. You must be open to changing your direction over and over again until the right road appears for you."

My words seemed foreign to her. They were different from anything she had ever heard. She listened intently. "Cancer and willingness are the lessons," I told her. "What's happening to you is a gift. At first glance, the packaging of this 'gift' seems ugly—something to be feared. But what started out as pure fear will turn into the greatest lesson of your life. The more you look inside yourself, the more you will realize how valuable this experience truly is. It is the gift of life, not death. Always know that God would never have given you such an advanced lesson had he not believed in your ability to achieve an excellent outcome."

I explained to Carmen that I would help guide her back to health. I was not going to do it myself; I could not do it *for* her. *She* was responsible and would have to take a large role in her own healing process. I reassured her that we all have the ability to heal ourselves by bringing ourselves back into balance. She was ready to accept this, and she did.

Carmen's greatest challenge was trust. Trust and safety were foreign words to her. She wondered how could she ever trust her body again after it had let her down. She didn't feel safe in her own body; she didn't feel safe in her own life.

Carmen worked with me for two years. We met weekly and I guided her through powerful spontaneous *interactive realizations*, because there is always dual responsibility between my patient and me. My patients actively participate and are completely involved in the process.

Sometimes we visualized traveling into places within Carmen's own body, reconnecting and reacquainting herself with her immune system. Another time, I guided her far away from her life and she became a tree. She went through a natural change of seasons, and as the leaves fell from the tree, her cancer cells fell easily and lovingly from her body to create space for new, healthy cells.

RECLAIMING THE GIFT OF WELLNESS

As Carmen became more proficient at proactive living and more open to learning from her own mind and body, she eventually felt safe enough to reclaim her right to live and to open the gift of wellness. We cleared pathways for her physical body to breathe emotionally again and this strengthened her. We used every medical treatment she was undergoing as a tool to strengthen and improve the quality of her life. It was working.

Even during the process of chemotherapy, she gained authority and confidence in her own life. We created a way to use every situation in her life as a catalyst to lead her to health. We saw her chemotherapy as light energy, and I told her that darkness could never live in the presence of light. When the sun comes up in the morning, all darkness disappears. As I guided her into her body, I showed her that all of her healthy cells were day cells—filled with light—and her cancer cells were night cells. As soon as the chemotherapy (light energy) reached her cells, the dark, sick ones would turn to light. It wouldn't harm her healthy cells, just make them brighter. I taught her to visualize that the chemotherapy could only do good in her body.

As she shifted her consciousness in so many shapes and forms, she created clearer, stronger and healthier ways of thinking and living. The more she *took* for herself, the more she became. Carmen had been in a committed relationship with her boyfriend, Bob, for years. They had been living together. Although she loved him, things weren't quite right. As in many relationships, years passed and nothing changed. As she approached her life with more confidence, she realized she was no longer willing to compromise what she felt was important. She asked Bob to move out and to not contact her for a few months. She needed time alone to reflect.

At first the loneliness was uncomfortable. But the more time she spent alone, the more she realized what was most important to her in life.

LESSONS IN LIFE

Carmen was aligning her internal world with the external world she was living in. She soon realized that the lessons she was learning were not lessons in *cancer*, but lessons in life. As her confidence grew, she became certain that her cancer was healing. She was growing in ways she never thought possible before. She felt as if her options in life were unlimited. She trusted her choices, and all of her relationships were improving.

After a few months, Bob phoned her. "I miss you so much, Carmen," he said. "Could we at least meet for dinner?" She chose to go. He had also been doing some inner work, cleaning up all the old things that were holding back their relationship. They dated for a couple of months to be certain that things were indeed different. They really were, and with each visit their hearts grew stronger and closer.

Carmen learned that as she changed, her whole world seemed to change with her. She no longer focused on her old negativity. Her new positive perceptions and beliefs were creating closeness in her life. Bob moved back in. Her friends were seeing Carmen as a role model and were seeking her advice and counsel. She was not only connecting to her own life, she was gaining a more profound awareness and a deeper trust toward God, the universe, and herself.

TAKING CHARGE OF SELF

After she completed her chemotherapy treatments with her medical doctor, he said that he had changed his original opinion about surgery. Whereas before he said surgery would do no good, now he insisted on following up the chemotherapy with a mastectomy. At this point, Carmen was uncomfortable with his suggestion. She declared that she was healed. He looked at her with disbelief and said, "It's impossible for a tumor the size of yours to be gone. If we do not do this mastectomy, you will die."

She said with calm conviction, "How dare you say that. You have no right to make that decision or to try to intimidate me. You're supposed to be on *my* team, in support of *me*.

"Before I go any further with your recommendations, I insist that you run some tests to see for certain where my so-called tumor is." Her doctor reluctantly agreed and did a spiral biopsy throughout her entire breast.

A week later, Carmen ran into my office bubbling over like a champagne bottle that had just popped its cork! "My pathology report came back NEGATIVE!" she said, jumping up and down.

"What did your doctor say when he read the report?" I asked.

"You're not going to believe his reaction. He said, 'We probably missed some of the cells. I'm sure your tumor is still present.' Dr. Jill, it's almost as if he didn't want to believe it's possible that I healed so well."

"I don't think for a moment that it's not that he doesn't want you to be well," I said. "It's just that his medical training and *statistics* have trained that faith out of him. What did you do?"

"I stuck to my guns and asked him what type of test *would* completely confirm my condition. He suggested a CAT scan. So I agreed."

A few days later the results were in. Once again, Carmen ran into my office, this time holding the X-rays with joyful tears flowing. No tumor was evident. She was clean.

BEHIND THE SCENES PARTNER

Carmen had worked extremely conscientiously and had focused on her life, not her disease. Now, the day after my dream, when we had finished writing her story, my stack of papers caught her eye.

"What's all that?" she asked.

Of all people, Carmen would understand the significance of the messages I had been hearing and writing. I smiled at her and said, "This is the newest information that's been revealed to me. I haven't even read it yet. Want to look at it together?"

"Absolutely!" We read the first words and looked at each other with amazement.

"Wow," she said softly.

We shall remain partners now and forever

You lead and I shall follow.

Within this lifetime you remain in the spotlight
and I will support your choices from behind the scenes.

What you bring to me I will see as truth.

The impact of these statements left us both speechless, and we pondered them for a long while. "Carmen," I declared, "this changes the whole picture. Our truth always wins! Regardless of what that truth is."

Thinking out loud as she spoke, Carmen finally said, "You know, that sounds so new to our ears, but when I think about my life, I think that's the way it's been. As you have been showing me, whatever you put in you get out. Remember when my well was so dry? No one ever got a cool drink out of that empty reservoir, I can tell you!"

"You were so dehydrated on the inside, and God kept trying to signal you through your emotions and your symptoms . . ."

"And I wasn't listening, and things got worse and worse, but when *you* helped me open up that whole new way of thinking—that I could actually *choose* to fill myself up with good things, my well began to overflow with health and love. I could truly say, "my cup runneth over."

"You're a perfect example of my input-output theory! God is always there—always our partner. If you decide to run around the block, your heart will follow and speed up. If you choose to slow down and rest, your breathing will follow and slow down. Whether you choose health food, junk food or no food, your body will only digest what you put into it. God can only take the lead from your choices. Your body never knows what you *don't* introduce into it;

your body can only work with what you deliver. God is a helping hand, not your feet; you have to do the walking."

Then it hit me. *"Carmen, this is another lasting impression! The soles ("SOULS") of our feet!* God put our "soul" on the bottom of our feet so we can make our own lasting footprints in the sand to remind us to always choose the direction of our path. Whatever energy we deliver to our inner partner will create our outcome. We choose the quality of contribution we bring into our life."

"We really *do* have the leading role in our life. We are the stars!"

We were awestruck by this awareness. We felt so liberated. We felt so loved.

It was time for my next patient. Carmen and I hugged. We were both very aware that we had shared something incredible. As Carmen walked out the door she looked back at me and said, "I will always take the lead and take full responsibility and make excellent choices for my life. I am still going to be open to learning, but from now on, I choose not to learn through cancer anymore! *I choose life!"*

She has indeed chosen life. Carmen is still learning and living cancer-free now, three years later.

The Gift
of Choice

You now and forever

will be a true

representation

of the capability to access

all divine manifestation.

You are a self-fulfilling prophecy

that is dictated

by your choices!

I Can Reclaim My Life

Carmen's powerful presence still filled the room, even though she had left. She had unburied her treasure, her life, by uncovering the gold of life-enhancing choices. What a perfect example of a woman who had taken over the director's chair of her own life's story!

I became aware that I was still holding the unread pages of my revelations scribbled down so passionately from the night before. How I wished I had just a few minutes to read on. The phone rang. It was my next patient, telling me she was running late, and this gave me the time I needed. Everything always works out! I read . . .

> *You are capable of so much more*
> *than you realize!*
> *You are participating in a joint venture of co-*
> *creation. You are not in this game alone. There are*
> *guidelines to follow and strategies for success.*
> *The complete HOW-TO MANUAL lives within each and*
> *every one of you. Your body has been chosen as your*
> *headquarters for learning. It is a sacred space that is tem-*
> *porarily leased—a place that must be honored, respected*
> *and nourished with energy. The space will thrive only as a*
> *direct reflection of a balanced partnership.*

I was beginning to feel as if I were in a spiritual business partnership with God, and *my* body was the space being leased to bring these messages forward. As I continued to read, I could barely make out the next words in my scribbled writing—"Spirit . . . innate . . . three energies . . . ?" When I figured it out, I was amazed: It was actually telling me what my spirit is composed of!

Your Spirit is pure energy in motion. There are three harmonious aspects of this energy, each with individual responsibilities: Innate Intelligence, Thought, and Emotion.

1. The First Energy of a Spirit is
INNATE INTELLIGENCE,
which is 100% God's
responsibility.

My responsibility in our contract is the automatic power that runs and replenishes your body constantly and continuously. It is the same energy of universal intelligence that runs our world, rotates the planets, and regulates the seasons and the cycles of day and night. As this powerful energy feeds into your body, each individual cell renews itself, giving it meaning and purpose. As in every form of life, as each cell fulfills its purpose, it goes through the natural progression from life to death. The innate energy will stay attached to the cell only as long as the cell is useful to the body. When it no longer serves a purpose, it will be replaced with a new one.

Your inner world mirrors the world you live in. You can live in the world that supplies the energy that allows the sun to rise and set, but you cannot have power over it. Likewise, you are a part of life's natural process, with the ability to direct only your own viewpoint as you interact with others—you may not try to control them.

This made perfect sense to me and echoed what I had learned in my training. But what followed took me into new territory.

Innate intelligence runs automatically, although it must operate in conjunction with direct signals from your choices and actions; it will obey them. You are the master of your mini-universe within; your inner spirit depends completely upon your contributions. You are to direct the world that lives within you and integrate it with your outer world. In this way, the God source of energy within you is used for the purpose of private soul-creating lessons.

What? I get to take a piece of universal creation and work it privately within me? I was enthralled with this idea of a private school for my soul, but I was also hesitant about having this much responsibility. Then I caught myself. I reminded myself that I also have a lot of help; after all, I'm partners with the Divine! A feeling of leadership, power and mutual trust came over me. All at once, I felt more space and freedom of spirit than I had ever known. I knew my soul had just expanded to a higher level. Ready to infuse my mind and soul with more new information, I read on.

2. The Second Energy of Spirit is THOUGHT,
which is 100%
YOUR responsibility.
Your responsibility to our contract is feeding your body with soul food with energy. That energy source is your THOUGHTS. Every thought you create directly affects our partnership and the quality of your life. How our two energies relate to each other will determine the quality of regeneration and replenishment.

You volunteered for this experience, therefore all voluntary functions are your responsibility. This is your only means of contribution to your sacred space—your body. You guide by your choices and I will always follow your lead.

*Think of it as holiday time all year 'round. You
receive many gifts for being in this life experience. You
decide the quality of the gifts you want to receive.*

*You are a self-fulfilling prophecy that is dictated by
your choices.*

My mind was stretching in every direction. I was learning that I can participate in the process monumentally, but I can't control what's outside of me. What I *can* control is me and what I feed into my own body. I'd better have some quality thoughts and make some quality choices if I want good results!

*We work hand-in-hand. Our responsibilities are unique
and different. Our energies complement each other,
but do not replace each other. Do not put your responsibilities back into my hands or assume that my responsibilities are yours. Do not blame me or give me all the
credit. I will always do my part and trust that you are
doing yours. As equal partners, we must contribute
together in order for this joint venture to succeed. I gave
you freedom of choice. Exercise it joyfully.*

Oh, my gosh, I was thinking, we so often relinquish our responsibility for getting the results we want. We say things like, "It's all in God's hands" or "I'll let fate decide." We either act like victims, or we don't want the responsibility. We're afraid that we don't have enough control, when, in fact, we do! I was feeling more powerful by the minute, and I could almost feel God smile.

My mind was swirling with all the thoughts I had just read. This was an opportunity for us to turn around our entire way of thinking! My revelations confirmed that we truly are meant to take control of our own lives. They also make it clear that if we keep an open mind, we are opening up to accessing God energy within us, and that's how we work together in harmony—the "quality" of our partnership. Beautiful.

MASTER CONTROL

You came into this world with the master control—your thoughts. They are your vehicle to success. Every voluntary action and feeling in your life will be initiated by a thought. What you believe, so will you become. You are your thoughts; you are what you think about. As you feed yourself thoughts, you create a life built upon your choices.

3. *The Third Energy of Spirit is EMOTIONS,*
   the communication system between
   you (your thoughts) and
   God energy within you
   (innate intelligence).

This energy is a coalition of the first two, and acts as a gauge to help you achieve the results you desire. Thought energy is sent into the body and sparks a reaction with innate energy to create the energy of emotions. This establishes a central communication system between thoughts and involuntary bodily functions. It is the way your inner self communicates with you. It is your biofeedback program. It is a pain and pleasure system that helps you balance your thoughts and gauge how you are evolving.

If you are not in a growth state of mind, you will be given a sign or a signal to change. Change is mandatory. There will either be a reason or season for change. You will either find the reason to naturally change yourself or I, your inner partner, will assist you by finding a reason for you to make appropriate changes. You may

> find yourself receiving a signal from an emotion, a phys-
> ical symptom or illness, or from reactions from others.

Our emotions talk to us and give us important clues! I always thought I didn't have any control over my emotions, but now I realized that I do. I must pay attention to them and honor them, or change my emotions through my thoughts and by my choices.

> *Emotions are feelings. Feelings are the eyes of the soul, creating the inner sight within you to report to you the condition or desirability of the thought you are feeding your soul. This question should always be asked: "Does that thought or action nurture and support me?" Your emotions and your body's reactions will tell you. Feelings enable you to dictate your own journey.*

How can I tell if my emotions are serving me? I wondered. *How can I tell where they are directing me?*

> *Life is filled with challenge and reward—also known as void and fulfillment. Every action in life provokes a feeling. You can shift, change or recondition your thoughts or actions in response to the feelings they create. By doing this you can realign or adjust your motives, thoughts and actions in order to produce desirable outcomes.*
>
> *This emotional magnetism is a two-way energy. Your emotional reactions, in addition to traveling back to your thoughts, simultaneously radiate to the world as a reflection of who you are at that moment. In this way, you receive feedback from the world regarding the signals you are putting out. The world will support that energy as truth and bring you acknowledgment in the form of an experience.*

So much to think about! I had always thought that emotions were private—that I owned them. But now that I thought about it, of course our emotions affect others. If I get upset, it affects my whole family. Everybody reacts. I was beginning to imagine my emotions acting as my trusty courier. I send out emotional energy and it brings back lessons that reflect the energy I transmitted. This means I'm creating my own reality, minute by minute, choice by choice.

I could see it. Like attracts like. Many times when I've felt on top of the world, I've entered a room and seen the sparks fly! People who also felt good came up to me, we'd bounce off each other's positive energy, and soon others would join in. At other times, maybe I'd be feeling low or depressed. I wouldn't even say a word, but others would feel it. They'd ask what was wrong, or simply put their arms around me. Or maybe someone else who was depressed would come over to commiserate or complain—you know the saying, "misery loves company." What we put out is what we get back.

I suddenly understood that my emotions were acting like a magnifying glass, reflecting my needs from my very soul. It impacted me, for I knew now that when my eyes lit up with happiness or shed tears, when I cried or raged, my soul was doing the same. I could almost feel the eyes of my soul staring straight into my own. A tear signified that I completely felt the connection.

As I feed thoughts to my soul, it digests them, creates a feeling to clue me in, and leads me closer to my greatness. *Another lasting impression—emotions are my steering wheel!* Now I know that I'll never have another feeling without recognizing that my soul is sending me insight so I can feed it properly.

It's so amazing how the right people come into our lives at exactly the right moment to confirm or realign our current thoughts. Here

I was learning about emotions, when my next patient, Alice, walked in, barely holding back her tears. By her own testimony, Alice was a wreck. Her steering wheel of emotions had steered her into a collision. She came today hoping I could help her feel safe again.

TRYING TO BE PERFECT: ALICE'S STORY

"I just want to go home, back to Indiana. This city life is not for me."

But it was not as simple as going home. Alice's story is much more complex than that. Alice had moved to Atlanta from a small town where she was raised by her mother in a cocoon—her mother's way of trying to compensate for her father's absence. Alice's mom tried hard to make everything perfect for her daughter. Alice became a perfectionist and an overachiever. Always trying to please, she couldn't do enough. She was an honor student, a talented ballet and tap dancer, a gymnast, a cheerleader, and the chair of the yearbook staff. Her popularity and achievements created a feeling of safety for her. After graduation, she entered a college in her hometown and remained in the safety net of her friends, and, of course, her mother.

Alice looked perfect on the *outside*—tall, thin and beautiful, well-dressed and well-spoken. But on the *inside*, something was always tugging on her heartstrings. She wondered what life would be like outside her cocoon.

After graduating from college, she took a chance and moved to Atlanta. Out of her safety zone, she felt uncomfortable. *People are so different here,* she kept thinking.

So she retreated and spent a lot of time alone. She was very homesick until she met Steve, a local man who had roots in the area. They fell in love and married. Now she had an anchor.

Alice felt more secure, but when Steve wasn't around, her self-confidence wavered. She depended on his companionship for her own fulfillment. When he was around she was happy; when she was alone, she wallowed in her past memories, making Atlanta seem more overpowering and unworkable. She created thoughts: *In Indiana, it's easy to make friends; in Indiana, I always fit in; in Indiana, I felt safe and powerful; everything here is big and overwhelming.* Alice was always blaming the big city. It never occurred to her to consider that what wasn't right might be inside herself. Her whole world was beginning to feel unsafe, out of control. Then one day she hit rock bottom.

She was out jogging couple of miles from home. She turned the corner and suddenly felt anxious. She panicked and started breathing rapidly. She looked around and thought, *if something happens to me, no one will be here to help me.* She fell to the ground, hyperventilating. She was having a severe panic attack. Fortunately, a young man who was jogging behind her saw her fall and helped her home.

After that, the fear really set in. Alice became so afraid that she wouldn't leave home alone. Throughout her days, fear and desperate thoughts occupied her time. *What if I panic again and no one comes to help me? What if I look bad—what will people think of me?* Her fears became addictive, demanding constant attention. She was tiring fast. Then one day it hit her: *Maybe it's not Atlanta; maybe it's me.* This was Alice's first sign that she was stepping onto the right path. Still, she felt there was no way out of her mess. All she could do was blame herself and live in self-pity.

ANGELS AT WORK

Steve suggested that Alice seek therapy, and she was more than willing to try it. She met with a counselor and over time gained enough trust in herself to go back to work—her only venture out alone. Alice had gone from being a popular, "I can do anything" person to being someone who considered going back and forth to work a major accomplishment! And who should Alice be working for but one of my patients, Vicki! As soon as Vicki learned what Alice was going through, she called me and made an appointment for her.

FINDING HER TRUE HOME

When I first met with Alice, she kept repeating "There's no place like home," like Dorothy in *The Wizard of Oz*. She longed to return to Indiana, but explained that moving would be a hardship for Steve, who owned a successful local family business. Alice was confused because she loved her husband, yet yearned for the peaceful feelings Indiana represented.

I asked her, "Do you really want to go back to Indiana, or do you want to feel comfortable and safe anywhere you live?" Without hesitation she said, "Of course, if I could create comfortable feelings *here*, I would. I want to feel safe here with Steve. I'd be the happiest girl alive!" Then she added sadly, "But it seems impossible."

I could see the true home she was longing for—safety within herself.

TAKE A BREATH

I asked her, "How peaceful would you feel if I could say one simple word that would help put you back into the driver's seat of your life, and help you to feel safe again?"

She looked at me with disbelief and said, "If you could do that, I'd feel . . . well, wonderful!

I smiled. Then I whispered, *BREATHE*.

She looked shocked. "You're kidding!"

"No, I'm not. Try it. Breathing is our connection to our inner self.

The most essential way to relieve anxiety and get back into choice is to remember to . . . *breathe!* Take a deep breath."

She breathed in deeply and relaxed visibly. I had noticed before that her breathing was fast and shallow. It wasn't feeding her body vital oxygen and that was contributing to her alarmed state.

"Panic is just another word for an emotion that's produced when a person feels out of control. Your emotions came from your belief that you are not safe and secure. Soon your thoughts were overwhelming, so your emotions alerted you that you were getting out of balance."

"How did this happen?" she asked.

"Like many of us, you didn't know how to interpret your emotions or use them in a positive way. Instead of growing and learning from these feelings of discomfort, you panicked and resisted change. You either ignored your symptoms or escalated them.

"Alice, the signals always get stronger until you *must* pay attention and make some changes. You finally got to the point where you could no longer ignore your signals. They literally knocked you down."

I continued, giving her some insight about her childhood "cocoon."

"When you try to live in a 'perfect' world, it can get pretty tricky. If you believe that there is only one right way to live, then there is no room for change. Anything outside of your familiar ways will never be good enough. When we get on this endless cycle of *I have to do more and more to get it right,* we become lost in a maze that keeps getting more overwhelming. Is that how you're feeling right now?" She nodded.

"Being an overachiever is fine, as long as your life is balanced and you're not afraid of change. Now I'm going to lead you to an awareness that will help you turn your way of thinking around. Give your-self a gift—take a deep, cleansing breath and exhale." She did.

"How did that feel?" I asked.

"Wonderful!" Alice replied.

"Taking that breath was a choice. You chose to think of that breath with the word 'gift' attached to it. That will make a difference. And remember, breathing in and out is a flowing exchange. Just as you can pause and take a breath, you can also simply pause and exchange your thoughts. It's as easy as breathing."

RECYCLING OLD THOUGHTS
LEAVING ROOM FOR THE NEW

"When it comes to our physical body and our spiritual energy, we perform that exchange process perfectly, just as when we breathe naturally. But when it comes to our 'same-old' thoughts and emo-tions, we don't do quite as good a job, and we fall down." I could see that Alice was starting to feel safe with me. She was ready to hear my next words.

"When we hold onto things that no longer work for us in our lives, we leave no space for the new. Alice, the breath you took that day when you were running and panicked is the *same* breath you took just now when you felt safe. The only difference between the two was your *choice of thoughts* at the time. One breath you associated with fear; the other with safety. All of our thoughts, even thoughts about resisting change, are choices we make.

"Here's your gift: *You have awareness now.* You will never have a thought again without knowing that you are actually choosing it and creating your life! You alone have the ability to challenge each thought and create space for a new one . . . to create a new destiny."

Making the Change:
How to Regain Emotional Balance

Alice said, "O.K., so now I'm ready to leave space for the new and turn this problem around. But how can I do that?"

I replied, "There's a very simple exercise you can practice to reclaim your life. Remember, all emotions are by-products of the quality of your thoughts. First, think of your negative emotions as "dirt."

Exercise: The Cup of Life—Pour in What You Want to Become.

I took a clear cup and poured clear water into it. "Pretend that this cup is your body. It is a container that you lease in order to learn and grow in this lifetime. It represents your life. The water in the cup is your spirit—the energy that fills it up. Your spirit must supply energy to your body (your sacred space) so that your body can work and renew itself—renew its 'lease.'

"At birth, the water inside your body is pure and clear. Over the years, you add thoughts—some positive, which show up as more clear water, and some negative, which appear as dirt." I grabbed some dirt from a nearby flower pot, threw it in the water, and shook it up. "Here, at the bottom of your cup of water, is your childhood dirt. Floating throughout your cup is the dirt you accumulated over the years, and at the very top of your cup is the fresh dirt you just added yesterday."

Alice said, ". . . like the way I felt when I was fighting with Steve last night . . ."

"Exactly," I said. "So many patients come to me and say, 'I can't believe what's coming out of my mouth! I know what the right thing is but I can't seem to do things differently.' It's as if all our broken dreams, old thoughts and negative ways are on display, overflowing from our cup for the whole world to see! They become mud in our cup. So now, instead of having a pure, fresh cup of water, your life's solution appears to be a muddy mess."

Cleaning Out the Mud

"Most people believe that if they could get rid of that 'dirt,' they could be happy. Alice, the truth is, you cannot just get rid of it. Once you have created that muddy solution, that is who you are at that moment. You are all of it. The only way to make a change is by changing the solution as a whole."

We walked over to the sink; I turned on the water and grabbed some more dirt.

"Your cup of life is constantly replenishing itself: good thoughts, add more clear water; negative thoughts, add more dirt. Picture the clear water and the dirt pouring continually at the same time—insecurities, loving acts, fears, kindness, confusion, growth, angry reactions—and mixing together.

Alice said, "I get it. On just one day, my solution could be made up of emotions such as pride—I got out of the house and made it to work; meanness— I was mad at a co-worker who annoys me; fear— I got out of breath, then berated myself for doing it; love—I love my husband and I let him love me."

Diluting the Solution

"Yes! The only way to change the solution—your life— is by putting into it what you want it to become. If you keep adding more clear— good thoughts—your cup will overflow and begin to dilute. The overflow is how you show up in the world right now. As you add clear thoughts, you'll still see old spilling over, but you'll also see evidence of the new.

"Your responsibility is to keep adding into your life thoughts about what you want to become, until eventually you are filled with exactly what you want to be. If your whole life is muddy, it's hard to notice when you add more dirt. When your solution is clear, if even one drop of dirt enters, it will stand out obviously and you'll easily notice where you need to make changes.

"How can I resist my old feelings and thoughts?" Alice asked. "I'm so used to thinking this way."

THE LAW OF ATTRACTION AND EXPANSION

"Now it gets a little bit tricky," I explained, "because of the law of attraction and expansion: *Whatever lives within you now, you will long for even more.* Whatever you say, think, feel, or eat—and the ways you act right now will expand as a part of you. You will crave more of the same. But in order to make a change, you must resist wishing for things that you really no longer desire, and add into your cup the things you want instead, even if it feels fake or uncomfortable at first. *Your focus must always stay on the input.* As you keep adding new thoughts to your cup, the new will expand within you, you will demand more or these new thoughts, and they will become part of you. We must take our focus off our problems and put it on creating new thoughts instead."

Alice thought for a moment and then said, "So instead of filling my cup with words and thoughts about how I dislike Atlanta and wish I were in Indiana, I should fill my cup with thoughts of how happy and healthy I am here, and what wonderful things are happening for me—even if they aren't happening yet."

"Right. Picture your cup of muddy water changing. Stop putting in negative thoughts of fear and pity and change them to positive thoughts of trust, inner peace, and patience. Your solution will start diluting and you will see immediate evidence—your new truth."

USING YOUR NEGATIVE EMOTIONS TO HELP YOU

"Now for the next step," I continued. "We're going to use all of those negative thoughts and emotions to lead you back home to a state of inner peace and a feeling of control. What I ask you to do is to understand that whatever you are feeling in your life is a lesson and a blessing. Now give yourself the greatest gift in the world—the opposite of the feelings that you do not like. So, if you feel fearful, this is phenomenal news! This means you are on the way to feeling totally safe wherever you are.

"Any feelings that you were born with make up the true, inherent energy of your spirit—love, trust, acceptance, willingness, inner direction, determination, self -acceptance, personal power— all the good traits. Everything else is a learned behavior—it's not a natural energy of your soul, and therefore it can be unlearned. Alice, there's only one thing that I know for sure about your past: it's over!"

THE FORMULA FOR CHANGE

Here's the formula: *We must change our focus from the output to the input, and the solution will overflow and clarify naturally over time.*

Most people look at the results in their life—often disappointing ones they deem failures—and by focusing on them, they add "old thoughts" back into their cup. If our solution or our overflow is not what we want, we must add to it what we want it to become.

So every time you get a thought or emotion you would like to change, ask yourself: *Is this really a part of me, or did I learn it from someone else?* Here's an example:

RETRAINING OLD EMOTIONS

Childhood is not a bed of roses for many of us. Mine wasn't any different. But I learned that my childhood experiences were all lessons for my benefit. My parents married very young, and within four years they had three children. You can imagine the stress for this young couple! My father had a temper and was extremely impatient with us children. If we wouldn't go to bed, he'd get angry, screaming until we finally obeyed and went to sleep.

I was born a very shy, calm child, and I remained that way when I became an adult. When I had children of my own, sometimes I had difficulty getting them to sleep. Every night, seemingly from nowhere, a rumbling, impatient feeling formed inside me and I'd start screaming, "Just go to bed!" I'd yell louder and louder each night. Then one day my young son complained, "I hate nighttime!" That stopped me in my tracks. I thought to myself, *I'm doing to my kids the same thing my dad did to me.*

I asked myself, *Are you an impatient, angry person?* The answer was clearly *No, I am not.* I realized that I had learned this thought pattern from my childhood and had created this feeling from my past.

I decided to use my feelings of impatience and frustration to remind me of who I really was—a patient person. I was going to use the same thing that got me into this mess to get out of it. I was committed to make a change no matter what.

The next time the inner rumbling started, I took a deep breath and said, "Thank you, God, for giving me this feeling to remind me that I am really a patient person." I tried to talk calmly to my children.

Still, on many nights I lost my temper and yelled at them, only to catch myself and apologize, letting my children know that my yelling wasn't their fault and that I was trying to learn new ways. I tried again and again, always blessing the feeling as my reminder. I was committed to using this process until it worked.

Since I'd had this inner rumbling since childhood, I thought that it would always be there, but as time passed, it eased up and I became a little more patient. Two years passed, and one day my husband and I were driving in the car. He looked over at me and said, "Jill, I really have to acknowledge what you've done. You've worked hard, and nighttime has become pleasant for the kids and the whole family. "

At the very moment I thanked Danny, I realized that I never got the rumbling feeling anymore. I wasn't even sure when it had disappeared. The feelings and symptoms in our lives only stay to remind us as long as we need them.

Change Your Self-fulfilling Prophecy

I told Alice—as I tell all of my patients—that all truths and answers are within us. I'm not going to give you or tell you anything you don't already know already.

I could see Alice taking ownership of herself. A calm, controlled feeling came over her, taking the place of her anxiety. The "how-to manual" was becoming clearer.

I shared with her the pages I had read that morning about how we are all our own self-fulfilling prophecy, dictated by our choices. She thought for a minute, and then said, "My fears and negative thinking about the big city were actually creating my destiny of paranoia."

"Yes, you were a self-fulfilling prophecy of what you didn't want to be. Alice, I'm putting you back in the driver's seat of your life. I am going to serve as your coach to remind you of the wonderful person you truly are until you can remind yourself. Step by step, day by day, you will make positive choices to shape your new destiny. You will become your own self-fulfilled prophecy of what you *do* want to be, dictated by your new fresh thoughts! Your true power will surface once again and you will feel safe and alive."

Alice made a commitment to no longer fear her emotions. Instead, she would use them as her guide. She was already creating a powerful choice.

SILENCE BETWEEN THE BREATHS

I left her with this thought. "Have you ever noticed that when you take a deep breath, there is a space—a little silence—at the very top of your inhale, that leads you back into the exhale? And at the very bottom of your exhale is a little pause again, a silence that leads you back into your inhale?" She shook her head no.

"If we inhale and exhale, neglecting that silence in between—if we don't allow for that little space—we hyperventilate, and our whole body panics. Alice, please remember the silence between the breaths." She nodded, took a deep breath, felt the space, and exhaled.

When Alice left, I smiled with satisfaction. She was on the way to reclaiming her life and valuing herself again, this time in her new surroundings. I would be helping her in the coming weeks.

I thought about Alice—along with many of my other patients. Why do so many people believe that they are smaller than they really are? Why do we settle for less than we really want? I yearned to find a better way to help people to see their true value. For I knew that beyond their limitations was . . .

a treasure of worth, just waiting around the corner.

The Gift
of Worth

Your Soul is

Royalty descended

from the Almighty.

You are entitled to

all that exists

simply because you are.

Your potential is

infinite.

I'm Worth It All!

What was that sensation in the top of my head? It was unlike anything I had ever felt. My mind raced and I wondered if maybe I had pushed the limit. Perhaps being up for all these days had finally taken its toll on me. Was I getting sick? It was probably from sleep deprivation. I rested my head on my desk, but the feeling got stronger. I started to get scared. I was producing thoughts that were more fearful than anything I'd ever imagined.

GOING CRAZY?

What if something's wrong with me? What if my head explodes? Many times during the past five days, I deeply questioned myself: *Was this real or not? Is this feeling normal? Is this the flu? Or am I going crazy?* Just when it seemed that these scary thoughts had reached their height, an amazing thing happened.

VISION OF THOUGHT EXCHANGE

A very strange feeling came over me and my mind started going on autopilot. It felt like something took over, and I was watching myself from inside out. I began to observe more as a student than a participant. A magnetic sensation pulled straight up from the crown of my head, expanding farther than I could see. It was then that I got really scared and confused, but soon an even more incredible thing happened.

The magnetic energy pulled my thoughts of fear straight out of the top of my head. I felt an emptiness only for a moment and then suddenly calm dropped in. My whole body relaxed and my mind felt safe. *It's O.K.*, I heard.

As my thoughts exchanged with each other, I stayed very still and watched the process. I realized that I couldn't hold two opposite thoughts in my head at the same time. When I let go of fear, safety came in; when worry left, calm entered. I started to get comfortable and began to play with the process. I'd purposely think of something negative or worrisome, and then, sure enough, I could pull it out and exchange it for something positive or reassuring. When I resisted the exchange, my mind produced more of whatever I was thinking. The thoughts kept flying back and forth. An old thought left and a new one took its place. I was starting to get the knack of it. As I became one with this system, I realized something else: When my mind shifted, my body followed. Just as I couldn't hold two opposite thoughts at the same time, I noticed that couldn't hold two opposite emotions at the same time. When my mind went fast, my emotions went fast. As soon as I calmed my thoughts, my body relaxed. Fascinating. As the moments passed, it became clear. I was not sick or tired. I was being led once again.

THE WAY TO ENDLESS ABUNDANCE

I was elated. Here *was* a way to achieve abundance—a thought exchange system! The concept that my thoughts are my only contribution to my life was already deeply embedded within. Now this system was showing me how easy it can be to make powerful choices that completely affect my life. The system could become my means of creation. How priceless this system was!

As my thoughts kept exchanging, I saw my soul being nourished simultaneously. Quality thoughts were entering my soul and I was becoming a reflection of my new thoughts. As my choices fell into place, my self-worth began to emerge. Excitement came over me, and I realized that this wasn't just for me, it was for everyone! We are *all* connected to this system. Every thought is available to us. I was in a state of euphoria. How could we fail when we could feel all of the possible thought choices within the universe?

Exchange, I kept hearing, *exchange*. The sky was a candy store with an infinite number of glistening, shining thoughts for me to take. I was a child who had no limitations. The endless wealth of possibilities was available in total abundance and unlimited supply. There were more thoughts of love out there than I could ever take in; there was more inner peace and clarity than I would ever need. As I kept practicing this process, I felt no need to hoard, hide or be selfish with this exchange because I could feel the universe replenishing itself every time I took a new thought. I could feel that there was "enough" thought energy for everyone. There was enough for all!

I felt emotions welling up, thinking how easy it was to create and exchange all my own negative thoughts for positive ones. I began to cry with joy and sadness. Part of me was overjoyed with possibility, but another part felt the sadness of abandoning my old way of thinking. Nevertheless, I was thrilled to have come upon this system. Something familiar had birthed inside. I had found my point of power—of worth—and it was intensifying rapidly. The more I took the more I became!

It was exciting to think of sharing this concept with people who are stuck in their negative thoughts. I could show them a new way to choose and exchange ideas. How easy it would be if they knew that there was a *Thought Exchange System*. We don't have to think the same thoughts over and over, creating the same feelings and attracting the same old results we don't want—because the answer to success is standing right before us. We can exchange all the old for new and better!

I began to listen more deeply.

> *You have the power to exchange. Exchange is the same as change. All of life's treasures are in unlimited supply, but you alone have the ability to choose what to keep or exchange. You alone are the manager of this process of creating your life. You will always have a connection to access all thoughts and possibilities in our universe. You can choose to exchange thoughts from others as well as from God and the universe. Exchanging thoughts, knowledge and spiritual help is always available. In order for fresh thoughts to come flowing through, the doors of your mind must remain open.*

As I started to come back into a semiconscious state of mind, I reached for a sheet of paper and started writing.

THE 10%–100% RULE

I wrote: *10%–100% rule.* We come from 100% unlimited vision and get to play with 10% at a time. When spirit is confined to limited, the mind will also have limitations. We use only 10% of our brain. Before I could even ask why, I saw the answer: That's the challenge—

learning through our limitations to build more quality choices. How frustrating it would be for our minds to have complete access, understand how to house all thought possibilities, and yet not have the physical capability to use it.

In the physical, we are restricted to the limitations of our body. We can't fly from dimension to dimension. As spiritual beings living in the limited, we must get in a car and drive to where we need to go. Therefore, the power controls in our lives are set up on an exchange system. God takes away 90% of our brain capacity in order for us to stretch, learn, grow and build upon all life choices. Thoughts fly in and thoughts fly out, always creating space to bring in others to add to our accumulation.

RETIRE YOUR OLD THOUGHTS

We must always keep the good thoughts, the powerful, useful thoughts. When a thought no longer serves our needs in life, we must retire it and exchange it for a new one. Out with the old thoughts that keep us stuck! Create space to bring in others that are more worthy of us!

The mystery of our life is looking for the next clue to create our next thought. Our joy comes from the new information, the insights, awareness and realizations we didn't have before. We yearn to add more quality thoughts to our consciousness. Our choices, moment by moment, help us to discover what happens next. We learn, grow, and then test our knowingness.

LOOKING FOR EVIDENCE
A thought can be used in one of two ways. You can look for evidence that proves a thought is working for you in your life, or you can look for evidence that proves it is

*not. That train of thought creates your destiny. The road
you travel is your choice. As your thoughts enter your
mind they enter your soul simultaneously. Your responsibility is to learn how to recognize quality and relay
value into yourself. Once it lives within, you will have
the ability to notice it in others. You can only see
through the eyes of who you are.*

Your soul is royalty descended from the Almighty.
You are entitled to all that exists
simply because you are.
Your potential is infinite.

This awareness was incredible! *All of life's greatness is in unlimited supply.* We are entitled to everything simply because we exist! Our potential is endless. Why then do so many of us prevent ourselves from having, being or doing it all? If we have the power and know what we
want, why can't we implement those more compatible thoughts?

I took a deep breath and was ready to share with my patients
once more. My day is often filled with people who clearly understand what they want in life. They all want the same thing—everything that's good: health, happiness, inner peace, the feeling of being
useful and valuable, being understood and being prosperous. The
overweight people clearly want to lose weight. The workaholics want
to learn to slow down and relax. The confused people seek purpose.
*Everyone wants to find out how to create the **opposite** of the thoughts that
are keeping them stuck.*

ADDICTIONS TO THOUGHTS

We all know the answers. The needing to diet or exercise or taking
time to relax aren't the problems. This is the problem: *We are addicted
to the same old negative thoughts.* Without realizing it we continually

sabotage ourselves in some way or another. Pulling these familiar addictive thoughts back in keeps us feeling small—thoughts like: *I just don't have the willpower to lose weight; I can't afford to slow down at work or I might get passed up on that promotion; no use trying to figure out what I'm supposed to do in life, I guess I'll never go anywhere.*

Is it that we don't *want* to see the big picture? Or is it just that we all get so comfortable with our uncomfortable patterns? The answer, in all cases, is the same: *We fear change. We're so fearful of becoming uncomfortable taking the step required to make the difference that we prefer to stay where we are.* Our intentions are wonderful, yet we never achieve the results we want in life, so we end up with a world of people who are "stuck." People who would rather sacrifice their lives and deprive their souls than open their minds to living differently. I was greatly saddened by the thought of all those crying souls created from fear. Their self-doubt is stronger than their self-worth.

The rest of the afternoon, I worked with patients who, I could see, were victims of their own thoughts. I shared lessons and felt their resistance building. My frustration grew stronger. My next patient came for an adjustment.

RECOGNIZING YOUR WORTH WHERE YOU ARE: BEVERLY'S STORY

Beverly was unhappy and frustrated with her job. She clearly wanted to change.

"What's keeping you from looking for a new job?" I asked.

Self-doubt poured off her words: "Well, what if I can't find a better one? At least I have a job and I'm making a living." *She's settling for less than she could be,* I thought.

"Beverly, don't you realize that you spend half of your waking hours at your job?"

"I never thought of it that way."

"If you had no limitations and you could do anything, what would that be?"

Her eyes lit up, and without hesitation she said, "What I really want to be is a counselor. I'd love to help people. I want to guide people back to health like you do."

I asked her to explain what her present job was. Her demeanor quickly changed from inspired to dejected. Her head hung, her shoulders sagged, her breathing became shallow, and she said, "I place people in my corporation in jobs."

"How do you do that?" I asked.

"Well, I interview them to see where their strengths and talents are, and put them into positions where they can succeed."

"Beverly, you do exactly what I do! You're no different than I am." She perked up a little. I continued, "My job is to see the greatness in others and help them to recognize and use it. In a sense you are already doing exactly what you said you wanted to do."

I wondered whether it was really the job she was unhappy with or her inability to recognize her worth in what she was already doing? Sometimes we get so fixated on looking at things in a certain way that we forget that we can do our "life's work" anywhere, in any situation. It's all how you look at it.

I said, "Maybe you just haven't realized the importance of what you're already doing. You're helping people to be useful in life! I'm certainly not saying to settle for this job if you're not happy. What I'm suggesting is seeing the possibilities of your talents *wherever* you are, no matter what the job title is. By recognizing the possibilities, you can create the life you truly want. You're worth having the life of your dreams."

She looked at me in disbelief. She was starting to realize that she was putting more emphasis upon her job title than on acknowledging who she was in her job.

Maybe we all need to re-evaluate what value truly is. If we make our job, our relationships, or the car we drive define us, we're bound to fail. Our value comes from within—the way we honor ourselves and share our gifts in whatever we do. I gave Beverly an assignment.

"This week at work I want you to exchange your thoughts. Instead of seeing yourself in a tiresome job, exchange that with the thought of seeing yourself as the counselor you want to be. Every time you place people in new positions, acknowledge that you helped them to help themselves improving their lives in a productive way! *Act* the part and I promise you'll *become* the part, wherever you go and whatever you do."

Beverly wanted so much to believe my words. She was just lifting the cover off the gift box of worth and peeking inside. Yet her doubt remained strong and her resistance was great. I was feeling a bit discouraged. I stopped and questioned myself once again. Did I feel this way because I was tired, or was it a sign that a new awareness was about to come through? I didn't know until John arrived.

OH ME, OH MY!: JOHN'S STORY

John had been a patient for several months. He had difficulty recognizing his greatness. At work, at home, and in life, he always looked for approval from others to make himself feel bigger and better. When work was great, he was great, and when it wasn't he always took it personally, beating himself up emotionally. Like so many, he felt he wasn't being paid what he was worth. John was totally dependent on the outer world to build up and tear down his inner strength. He was particularly sensitive to the expectations and criticisms of his wife Jodi.

John and I had had many sessions building his self-worth and self-esteem. He'd come in, get his dose of confidence, and leave feeling powerful. Then he'd walk into the real world, break down, and come back to me for his next dose. I had given him homework. It was simple. All he had to do every day was write a list of how he felt when he was in power. Then he was to recite it aloud in front of a mirror. He knew that the only way these lessons would stick was by doing his "inner homework" himself. I hadn't seen John in a few weeks. He walked in frustrated and angry at the world. He complained about his boss, his job, how no one acknowledged his work—and how his wife clearly didn't understand him. He seemed to see himself as a victim in many areas in his life.

I stopped him abruptly and asked, "John, have you been doing your homework?" He gave me excuse after excuse as to why he couldn't do it—not enough time, tired at the end of the day, family too demanding, and so on. I could see he was getting anxious to start our work together. He craved some insight and encouragement from me, but much to his surprise, I gave him the opposite. I said firmly and clearly, "If you are not willing to do the work, I'm not willing to work with you. You're fired. You're no longer my patient."

He was shocked. I knew he wanted to stay, but I was not willing to be his temporary fix of confidence. My policy is to coach people into independence and never allow someone to become dependent upon me. John's shock turned to fear.

THE POWER OF RESISTANCE

The thought of losing my help was so painful that he literally begged me to continue working with him. "I'm ready!" he pleaded, "I'll do what it takes to turn my life around." I looked at him and smiled, for he had just revealed another secret of the universe— *resistance*. It was obvious that that's where the power lies. Maybe we must feel a bit of resistance, pain or discomfort to make a change. Just *maybe,* the only way to discover our worth is to feel resistance as we go through the old habits, making the stretch into the new.

"Stand up!" I shouted. As he stood, John looked almost military and his eyes focused on me as I continued. "We cannot expect to go on our merry way in life and easily change without working seriously on our thoughts. It's time to stop the stinking thinking! Are you ready to honor yourself?" I was beginning to feel like a spiritual drill sergeant.

"Like a soldier," he said. "Ready, willing and able." He saluted.

"Even ready to push through the fear of change? It's very scary. People use the feeling of fear consistently as an excuse, and all it does is prevent growth. Are you ready to stop using fear as an excuse, promote your self-worth and see your value?"

"Yes, ma'am." John sat down again.

"There is a deeper truth than fear. John, your thoughts are addictions. We are so fearful of abandoning our old thoughts that we maintain allegiance to them at any cost. We'll even sabotage our own personal gain, dreams and desires."

"Why do we do this?"

"Because these thoughts are familiar. We'd rather stay with what we know, even though we really know better, and even though it keeps us stuck. Then we end up swimming in a great big pool of self-doubt and self-pity. *Oh, me, oh, my, life is too hard and nothing's working.* Your beautiful soul is crying out to be recognized and honored. It's time to change."

"So what's the next step?"

"To realize that your negative thoughts are your way back. The resistance that you feel in your life is not the problem, it's your solution. John, we build momentum in our lives by using this resistance."

"What do you mean?" he asked.

"Have you ever played basketball?"

"I play all the time."

"When you bounce the ball toward the ground, what happens?"

"It bounces back, of course."

"Exactly. The only reason you were able to create that momentum is because you and the ball are creating a resistance force. Most people believe that resistance is something to run from. I'm here to tell you that you're running from the wrong thing. You're doing it backwards! Make believe you have a ball in your hand and it loses it's air."

"O.K."

"Now if you bounce the deflated ball, what's going to happen?"

"Nothing. It won't bounce back."

"Of course not, because the resistance in the ball is what you were pushing against. That's what was building your momentum. Resistance is where the power lies."

"You're right! So when I meet resistance, I shouldn't give up, but run toward it, bounce it and improve my game."

"Yes. You said you like to play basketball. How often do you practice?"

"Every day," he said proudly. "Uh-oh." He got it and grinned. "O.K., coach. What exercises can I do every day to get good at this game?"

DEPOSITING INTO YOUR SOUL BANK

"John, in addition to your other exercise—which I'm sure you'll now do without fail—I want you to picture your soul as a bank. Every day, think about what you want to contribute to your bank account to build your worth—self-worth. You must only deposit and internalize what you want your soul to accept. Whatever you believe is what your soul believes, and it accepts what you deposit as truth. Whatever thoughts you think, your soul thinks. The way we grow and become all that we choose to be is by adding thoughts, knowledge and lessons to our mind. That accumulation is a reflection of everything we are. What we put in, we can take out and use. That's what makes you valuable to your business isn't it? The knowledge that you learned in your trade?"

"You've been unhappy lately around money issues," I said. "Most people don't understand what money truly is. Do you know what it is?'

"Of course I do. What a ridiculous question."

SOUL MONEY

"Maybe money isn't what you think it is. I want you to think of money as a universal 'thank you' system. Inside of you, there is an accumulation of everything you ever experienced and learned, right? All this information becomes your value. When others have the need for that information or service, money becomes the exchange system.

"Here's a simple example. It's lunchtime and you're hungry. So, you go into your favorite restaurant and see on the menu just what you're looking for. You have the need, they have the product. You see the value of their product, order your meal, and then pay them because they helped you to meet a need. Our salaries for our work are thank you's for helping others to fill their needs. Similarly, as we add more information to our mind's repertoire, we become more valuable and life acknowledges us accordingly.

The key to success is focusing on continually inputting valuable information into yourself. If you do this, the money will follow. Doesn't everyone want to hire people who know and can do things that they can't do? As others recognize your value you get rewarded. You can be, do, or have it all. All you have to do is know what other people want to know. That makes you valuable! Isn't that why you're here today? You want to know what I know."

"You're right. I was focusing on my salary to define who I was at work. Instead, I'd be better off focusing on putting positive thoughts into myself and my work . . ."

"You will see yourself more positively—and so will others."

"You're saying the money will come automatically?"

"Absolutely—from the overflow of your positive changes! Whatever you believe you can learn will become your new expanded boundaries and what you are capable of becoming. You must also be willing to accept money. When someone sees something in you that they want to reward or acknowledge, just like a thank you, you should accept graciously. By refusing, you are discounting their worth and yours. John this is the order of success: Thought . . . action . . . money!"

LIGHTS, CAMERA, _____!

"Now here's where the problem lies. It's not the lights. We have the ability to see what we want in life. It's not the camera. We have the instruments. It's the . . . action! We all have good intentions, with amazing ability to create powerful thoughts. The problem lies in taking *action*. When it's time to take responsibility and take steps to make the changes, we stop. As soon as life gives us a little resistance, we think we are doing things wrong, so we stop. Then we blame work, family, friends, parents, all of it, and we stay in deprivation, never getting what we want."

GREAT INTENTIONS, FRUSTRATING RESULTS?

"Here's a simple formula: *Intentions = Results.* Sometimes, even when we think we're changing our thought patterns, we can't recognize that we're still in a rut because our old thoughts are so familiar and comfortable. One of the ways you can tell if your new thoughts are on target or not is to observe your results. *If your results aren't worthy of your intentions, then it's time to do things differently.* Remember that the resistance you will feel to these changes is where your power will come from. That's the clue to moving forward and becoming unstuck."

"What do you mean?"

STRETCHING THROUGH THE DISCOMFORT

"In order to create a powerful, 'comfortable' life, you must allow yourself to feel *uncomfortable* as you stretch and strengthen into your new ways."

"Can you give me an example?"

"Stand up again, and then bend down and touch your toes."

As he reached down, the backs of his legs stretched and he grabbed them and said, "Ouch!"

"If your goal is to create flexibility in your muscles, how are you going to get the stretch without going through the pain?"

"So if one of my goals was to become a freelance consultant— which is scary because I haven't done it before—I'd start exercising this intention by taking on smaller jobs one at a time until I stretched those freelancing muscles to where I was comfortable taking on bigger jobs . . ."

"You've got it."

STRETCHING TOWARD ABUNDANCE

"John, here's a word of caution. Many times we can't distinguish between feelings that prevent our growth and feelings that arise as we reach for our new ways of being. There's pain involved with both. There's a very fine line between feelings of deprivation and feelings that come from stretching toward abundance.

"What do you mean by deprivation?" asked John.

"Anything inside of us that blocks our growth. We so often interpret the pain of the stretch as bad and we stop. That prevents us from going further in life. We end up pushing away many good things because we can't distinguish between the two different feelings. Here's an example:

"Let's say you and I are sitting around watching TV one night. We're in a big beautiful home eating, drinking, having a great time, living in abundance. A commercial comes on about a poor child in a third world country who's emaciated, fearful, starving and in total deprivation. It's obvious that this child can feel the pain of need. He knows something is terribly wrong and he's in fear. As his body creates those feelings he's thinking, *this is painful, this is not good.*

"So we pick up the phone in all our abundance and dial 1-800-SAVE-A-CHILD. John, do you know what happens? Within a day or two, that very same child has been given massive amounts of food. He looks at the food, believing this is a good thing, and he immediately starts eating. He eats so fast he gets cramps and grabs his belly. He thinks, *this is bad, this is painful.* So, he pushes the food—abundance—away. His body interprets his pain as bad—in his mind pain means starvation and deprivation. That's what's familiar to him. This little child couldn't tell the difference between the two pains. But you can—with practice."

John said, "Wow. *That* is a new awareness for me. It's a different way of thinking, but I can see what you're saying."

"How many times in life do we do the same thing over and over and feel deprived? Then when something new and good is presented to us, our mind and body try to stretch toward the abundance, but we interpret it as pain and we push it away? We're not willing to feel the pain of growth. We become fearful of the change, because we still expect only failure or deprivation. How do you want to interpret these feelings? Do you want to live in deprivation? Or are you ready to feel and push through the stretching into abundance?"

"Boy, I'm ready. I'm tired of the old routine." There was new conviction in his voice.

STRENGTHENING TIME

"John, when we are challenged with change, it's our soul's way of making space so we can add into it what we want to become. We can add education, positive thoughts and all of the interpretations and realizations we get from our life's experience. The more we add, the more new dimensions we add to ourselves."

"Does it always have to be so hard?"

I grabbed a two-pound hand weight and instructed John to do twenty-five lifts. After he finished, I asked, "How did that feel?"

"Easy, of course."

"Do you think you could strengthen and tone your body by using those weights?"

"Of course not."

Then I reached for a thirty-pound weight. "Do twenty-five reps with this." After he'd lifted the weight a couple of times, I could see him start to strain and struggle. He did about five reps and then said, "Man, this is too painful." He caught himself and grinned. "For now . . . but with practice . . . "

The Avoiding-Change-at-All-Costs List

"Exactly," I said. "Sometimes we must go through the discomfort to achieve our goal—a more comfortable life. Ninety percent of the people on earth live in fear. They are so afraid of change that they'll avoid it at any cost, even sacrificing their own happiness. When opportunity approaches, they push it away as soon as the going gets tough."

John grabbed some paper and started taking notes.

"When anything comes along that means we'll have to make a change, the first thing our mind does is try to block it. We try to avoid change at any cost, so our initial reaction to the suggestion of change is, *forget it.* Deep down inside we feel that if we ignore what's happening in our life, maybe the situation will go away.

"Our next change-fighting weapon is the *excuse list.* We'll use any excuse to convince ourselves that taking advantage of a new opportunity will cause us problems."

"Why do we do this?" John asked.

"So we don't have to make the changes. We don't want the responsibility, so we keep ourselves small. We're afraid of failing, but we're also afraid of succeeding. We're afraid of the unknown. We're afraid of communicating our thoughts and being judged. We're simply afraid of doing anything different from what we're already doing because we don't believe we deserve anything more than what we already have.

I asked, "Do you believe you're in control of your own destiny?"

"Kind of . . ."

"Most people believe that they're not in control of their destiny—that their destiny is dictated by outer circumstance. Their attitude is either *I never do anything wrong—it's someone else's fault* or *I can never do anything right, so why bother?* Afraid of being wrong or looking different, they worry about what other people think of them, so they simply follow the masses to fit in. Even when others give good advice, they make the results sound bad because they're afraid to succeed. They use lines like *You don't know anything,* or *That could never work,* so when they fail, they can accept it as fate—*It wasn't a good idea anyway.* They settle for less than they're worth; they sell out on themselves. Some people simply reject all of life's opportunities." I glanced at John's paper. "What have you written?"

He read from his list:

1. Forget it (maybe it'll go away)

2. Excuses—all the reasons why we shouldn't change

3. Afraid—needing approval and acceptance

4. Resistance—rejecting suggestions to make changes in our life.

I encouraged him. "Look at the first letter of each of those words."

"They spell out FEAR!"

THE TOP 10%

"Would you like to be in the top 10% of the people in the world?" I asked John. "The rare few who know the secret formula to success?" He nodded.

"Number one, write this down": **R.A.R.E.**

R—*Responsibility*—You must be willing to accept responsibility for your own life. Do not pay attention to what anyone else says, thinks, or does! Only *you* get to choose what you want to believe about yourself and your life.

A—*Action*—You must be willing to do what it takes to make the changes.

R—*Recognize it!*—You must recognize what it is that you want in life. All of it. Set a new standard—that you'll strive to understand your true worth and value.

E—*Exercise it!*—Like everything else in this world, unless you exercise your options, they are worthless. If you had a million shares of a Fortune 500 company and you never cashed them in, they would be worthless. It's time to cash in all your options and see the worthy person that you have always been.

"How did I ever forget?" he asked.

"The reason we are all living in a 'what if' world hoping for the 'if only' is because we forgot how to put value on ourselves. We easily recognize the value in others and deny our own importance. We continually buy into thoughts that devalue us. Thoughts like *I don't have a lot of money . . . My job's not important . . . I don't have a good education . . . I'm not married to the right person . . . I had a troubled childhood . . .* **Therefore, I'm not worth much.**

OUR VALUE TAG

"Your life's experiences, including the 'bad' ones, will never detract from your worth. Here's an example. Let's say I was holding a hundred-dollar bill. How much would it be worth?"

Without hesitation John said, "One hundred dollars."

"Now let's say I took that hundred-dollar bill and crumpled it up, how much would it be worth?"

"A hundred bucks."

"What if I rip it in half and tape it back together?"

"Again, one hundred dollars—even if you rub it in the dirt with the heel of your shoe and make a great big mess out of it."

"Of course. Regardless of what we go through in our life, our experiences never take anything away from our worth. We are worth it all! What if I told you that you can put a tag on yourself stating what *you* think your value is, and that's how you will be perceived. That you have the ability to constantly set new standards for yourself regarding how you choose to be valued and treated in life. You could attach a tag of $50 or make it $50 million. If I went into a store and saw a beautiful painting with a price tag of $50,000, how much would it be worth?

"Fifty thousand dollars," he said.

"Of course. That's because someone said that's the value of it. Now *you* can choose to accept or not accept that the painting is that valuable. Let's say you agree with that value and buy the painting. You take it home and hang it up on your wall. How would you treat that painting?"

"I'd treat it as a valuable piece, take good care of it. Probably put a light on it—show it off."

"Yes, you would, simply because it was priced as a very valuable item. This same lesson holds true for assigning a low value to something. Let's pretend your picture is ruined in a fire. Now you're not as proud of it because it's a big mess. So you take it off the wall and decide to sell it in the next garage sale. You tag it once again; but this time the price is $10. Someone will come by, see that $10 value on it and accept it as the painting's true value.

"Many people devalue themselves constantly because they believe that their life experiences deflate their worth. The truth is that they do not! You don't own an experience. The only thing that you own is the thought or feeling that was created by that experience. When a boy goes down a slide on the playground, he doesn't own the slide. All he owns is the thoughts and feelings that were created from that experience. All too often, we believe that we own our past experiences, and we allow them to dictate our life.

"John, you now have the ability to choose the thoughts upon which you will build your life. The ones you don't use you can recycle in that great big garage sale in the universe! It's a place where all old thoughts can be renewed."

NO MATTER WHAT

"John, would you like to re-tag your value right now?" I asked.

"Sure, let's go for it," he grinned.

"There are three words we use that I call the lowest level of thinking. The first word is **NO**. 'No' is used to respond to every suggestion that we grow, learn, honor ourselves or achieve. We resist change with lines like *No, I can't do this,* or *No, that won't work, No, that can't be true.* Do you know why we do that? To keep ourselves small!

"The second word that we use against our best interest is the word **MATTER**. We find the problems in everything, using phrases like *You know what's the matter with that . . .*

"I guess I've been a 'matter' person all my life—always looking for problems."

"And why do we find fault and problems with everything?"

"To keep ourselves small."

"Right! The third word in the lowest level of thinking is **WHAT**. We use the word 'what' religiously. *What do you mean? What does* *everyone want from me? What I don't understand is . . . What I'm doing wrong is . . .*

"Guess that's how I think when I'm dealing with with my boss and Jodi."

"I call it the innocent denial of change. Why do we do it? To keep ourselves small. We use the *Nos* the *Matters* and the *Whats* throughout our lives because we are so afraid of honoring ourselves and growing. Then one day—unfortunately, it's usually later in our lives rather than earlier—we realize our worth and we're ready to make a change. Then all those years of keeping ourselves small turn into preparation for achieving the *highest level of commitment we can give ourselves.* **NO MATTER WHAT!** Then our lives turn into, *No matter what,* I am going to honor myself! *No matter what,* I am going to take care of me! *No matter what,* I am going to listen to my gut instincts and trust myself! *No matter what,* I will treat myself as the valuable person I know that I am! *NO MATTER WHAT!*

By now, John was fired up—committed to changing the way he thought before it was too late, no matter what. I decided to end our session by guiding him through an interactive realization. "John, when you follow me through this realization, I want you to hold the *No Matter What* commitment!" He was ready.

A ROYAL DESCENDENT

I instructed him to lie down on my table and to take a few breaths to relax. Then I began. "Picture your soul before you entered this world, way up high in the universe. Your soul is royalty. It is a descendent from the "Almighty on High." From the King of Kings . . . from whatever highest source of energy and creative power has meaning for you. Picture your royal soul unlimited, living in abundance and being an important part of the balance for our entire creation."

John saw his soul very clearly.

"Now picture this royal energy we call your soul searching for a new lesson, a new growth experience. See it wearing a crown, walking down to earth on a royal red velvet carpet coming from the sky. It's marching so eloquently step-by-step, straight toward you. This royal soul is making a choice to enter into your body to learn and grow, and it wants you to be its teacher. You have the honor of accommodating it with your home, your body."

He took a deep, cleansing breath and said, "Incredible—I can see it."

"When it gets close to your head, let me know."

"It's getting close."

"Picture an opening on the crown of your head. Like a baby's crown when it's born."

"I can see it. It's a beautiful golden circle."

"When your soul gets close enough I want you to invite it in with a deep breath. No need to force or convince it, just allow it to enter."

John took a very deep breath, and I said, "You have the opening, let it in!"

His soul dropped into his body. "John, something amazing is happening. The crown, the royal crown—I see it being placed on top of your head." His soul spoke through my words: "Now you are the King. You have control and I, like your child, shall listen and learn from your choices, your truth. I promise to align and obey. You are my leader, you are royalty."

I could see tears flowing from John's eyes. He remembered who he really was, not who he thought he was taught to be. His essence was glowing and alive. "Your soul can only hear *you*. It can hear your thoughts and words and see your actions. It is blind to anything or anyone else in this universe. Now picture your soul like a newborn baby—Prince Johnny. He is innocent, pure, whole and complete! Your purpose in life is to interpret all life's lessons and experience and send them inward only in ways that will honor him. You must send everything that you want him to become, so he can grow and learn. Remember, he can no longer hear the outside world; everything must go through you first to get to him. He can only hear *you!* Your purpose is to raise and nurture this beautiful child, this little Johnny. Be selective in what you send to him!"

He opened his eyes and got up. I hugged him.

"We came into this world with it all. Knowing who we really are. Royal beings! All children are born with unlimited vision. They haven't been told otherwise. Doctors even intuitively speak the words of truth, not realizing the true intent and meaning behind what they are saying." When John looked puzzled, I asked him to think back to when his daughter was born. He remembered clearly. He said that Jodi had been in labor for hours and that they struggled ceaselessly until that magical moment when the baby started down the birth canal.

"Do you remember what the doctor said at that point?" I asked him.

"Clear as day," he replied. "He said, 'Your baby is crowning!'"

"Yes, another *lasting impression—our crown*—right from birth, on the top of our head. The first sign of our worth is acknowledged. We march right down the royal red birth canal carpet into this world as beautiful royal beings."

"Thank you. Now it will be easier to remember who I am. "

"And always remember that everyone else you meet is also royalty and that there is abundance for all. The others you meet are running their own kingdoms as well as they can. Knowing this, we can honor others and live in harmony. We all are equally valuable!"

As John got ready to leave, I could see that he was feeling the warmth of the truths he'd discovered. And I was thinking about the mystery and challenge that were about to unfold for him.

How would the world view the newfound king?

The Gift
of Allowing

As my partner,

you stand as an original!

One of a kind,

you will shine upon the world.

I support every step that you take.

Trust and allow for yourself

and always allow for others.

The brilliant differences

of each individual

will collectively create

the Whole.

I Allow for Others as I Allow for Myself

My spirit was soaring along with John's. He was at last seeing himself as the newborn king, ready to take on the world. But was the world ready to receive him? The challenge for John now was to apply his realizations in the real world.

His cell phone rang. It was Jodi, who had hurt her back lifting their baby daughter. He asked, "Can you please fit her in?" I was amazed that I was still standing after five days of visions, but of course I said to send her right over.

I knew John's first test was about to come. Was he ready to stop worrying about judgment? How would he react when his wife arrived? His feeling of being judged by others was so strong. I truly understood that he, like many of us, interprets life through critical eyes because he was brought up in a world where so many wear judges' robes. We are trained right from the start: Beware . . . Judgment Day will arrive.

WHAT ABOUT ME?

Jodi walked through the door with her baby in her arms, as stressed as could be. I could see immediately how severe her back pain was. Her whole body was guarded and leaning to the right.

John, who was still flying high from his session, hugged her and the baby, then enthusiastically spouted off about some of his epiphanies. Jodi was in such distress, she could think of nothing else. She handed him the baby and cut him off. "Why is it always about *you?* It seems like every time I turn around I'm expected to see things *your* way! I need time for *me,*" she declared. "Take the baby home and I'll meet you there."

John was stunned. To his credit, the neophyte king managed a royal attempt at a response. "I don't blame you for feeling that way. I know I need to make some changes. I hope Dr. Jill can help you with your back." He scooted out with the baby in a hurry.

Jodi was surprised at his response, but the dam of pent-up frustrations still cracked open and the grievances came pouring out. "That will be just another broken promise! At Christmas, he asked for my wish list and all I wanted was time with him. He gave me a beautiful card filled with promises of walks on the beach, family dinners, romantic evenings. Now it's February and not one of those things has happened. Does he think we're the perfect happy family just because we show up all pretty on the Christmas card year after year?"

The tears came, and I gave her a tissue. "I feel so unloved. I don't know how I'm going to survive this relationship! Living with him is an emotional roller coaster ride!"

Jodi had been a single woman out in the business world for many years. She had high expectations of herself and of everybody else. She had always dreamed of getting married, and she had a picture-perfect plan in her mind of what her marriage would look like. Now she was married and the picture was looking way out of focus.

Happily Ever After . . . I Fix Him: Jodi's Story

"All my life I wanted a husband and children," Jodi began. "I stayed open to that possibility even though the years seemed to be passing me by. Then my dream came true! Here I was, in my early forties, and I met my Prince Charming. I was thrilled to marry John and have a baby. He was such a nice man. This could have been such a happily-ever-after story! The man of my dreams turned out not at all the way I expected. Why couldn't it happen the way I envisioned? We're so frustrated and stuck, but we just can't figure out why. He doesn't spend time with me or our baby. I see her following him around, so sad because he's not playing with her. I want him to take walks with me on weekends, which he never does because he's too tired and takes naps instead. I wanted those romantic evenings, but he never asks me out. I used to feel so powerful when I was single. Now I feel powerless—powerless to change him and our life together. On top of all this, my back is killing me!"

Hurting Inside and Out

I asked Jodi to take a deep breath and lie down so I could examine her back. "Feel these muscles that align around your spine on the left side? They're contracting like crazy. Complete spasms in your lower back. Your body is way out of balance and the pain is a symptom—it's trying to tell you something. Pain on the outside is a reflection of something hurting on the inside."

"I guess my emotions are tied up in knots. So why does that come out as back pain and not a headache or something?"

"Where your body hurts gives you significant clues. Your lower back is the central pivot point of your entire body. It holds your upper and lower body together. Therefore, your lower back represents support."

"Boy, does that sound right. I don't feel supported at all."

"I know you don't. However, depending upon John or anyone else to hold you up or keep your life together won't work."

"Obviously," she replied. I used gentle pressure to release the spasms in her back.

"Dr. Jill," she said, "this relationship is not at all what I had planned." Her voice reflected her bewilderment.

BEWARE OF PLANS

I said, "So you had A PLAN, did you? Another of my patients, Leslie, had a plan, too. Hers was also to find the man of her dreams and to be totally committed to this one true love. When her relationship ended bitterly, her new plan was to put men on hold and not let anyone get too close.

"One day, she came running into my office, out of breath. I thought something terrible had happened and asked her what was wrong. She said, 'I've met a man!' She sounded so distressed that I sympathized with her: 'Uh-oh, and he's mistreating you?' 'Oh, no, I'm crazy about him and he's crazy about me. He's wonderful.' I asked, 'What's the problem then, for goodness' sake?'

"She said, 'He's not in my plan!' So I pointed out to her, 'Leslie, do you mean to tell me you are about to prevent true love from coming into your life because he wasn't on your list?' Leslie stopped to think about it. When she saw the humor in the situation, she laughed and relaxed. She let him into her life."

Jodi commented, "We can't just go through life without any goals at all!"

"Of course we must make goals. We just need to be flexible in the action steps to get there and in how the results show up. We never know how things are going to turn out. We just need to take it as it comes, or opportunities will pass us by."

THROUGH THE EYES OF PAST GENERATIONS

Jodi looked wistful. She said, "That story about Leslie made me think again about plans and dreams for relationships. My mother had a plan, too—that my father would love her deeply. That sure didn't work out the way she had envisioned. I always felt so sad for her. My dad loved us, but he worked all the time and Mom never felt appreciated or loved. She always complained and found fault with Dad, just like her mother before her complained about my grandfather. I did my best to try to comfort her. I knew how she felt. I wanted Daddy to spend more time with me, too. That made me determined not to have a marriage like theirs! At least my vision was different from my mother's."

"But, Jodi, look at how it turned out. You got the same kind of marriage your mother had!"

She looked shocked. The realization hit her. She said in a whisper, "I'm doing things just like my mother." This idea went straight to her heart, and she cried. "I've been finding fault with John. I've been so dissatisfied, so fearful that I wasn't going to get enough attention from him, the way I didn't from my father . . ." It was a lot for her to take in. Then she said in a small voice, "Oh, my gosh. I'm handing down that legacy to my daughter. Maybe she isn't sad. Maybe she's happy and I'm just projecting my sadness onto her." She cried, "Dr. Jill, how can I turn this around? I must stop this."

I said, "You've already begun. That's a huge awareness. We can go from there. Now that you're seeing with fresh eyes, you understand clearly what needs to be changed. That's a good thing! Now you can exchange those perceptions from your childhood with new ones. First things first. You grew up hearing your mother find fault with your father, and that's what you learned. You wanted to 'fix' your dad, right?" She nodded.

"You came into this relationship with John with high expectations of how you *didn't* want it to be, but ended up attracting exactly what you didn't want by looking at John through your mother's eyes, wanting to fix him, too."

She looked so forlorn. "I guess that's what I've been doing . . ."

". . . but you didn't know it. When we have such high expectations and they're not met, we find fault with everything and everybody. We try to change them and force them into our picture of perfection. When that doesn't happen, we make them wrong. It all comes from such grand visions, but we stray off the path in the execution of our dreams."

We looked at each other. We both got the significance of the word. We truly don't implement our dreams—we "execute" them—with expectations.

LETTING GO OF EXPECTATIONS

"John's always expecting so much of me, too," she sighed. "He always expects the house to be spotless, expects me to take care of the baby all the time, but he never pitches in to help . . . Oh, there I go again criticizing him. Just a minute ago, *I* was the one who was expecting everything of *him* . . ."

"Those expectations are killers. They turn us into judges. We have to let them go. Expect nothing and create everything."

"How on earth do you do that?"

"One thought and one action at a time. Never become attached to a specific outcome.

Dropping Your Weapon

"It sounds as if you and John are doing what many of us do. Spouses know each other very well, and know what they don't like about each other. We watch each other like hawks, and then we swoop down and attack to remind the prey of what they did or didn't do. Just like the Republicans and Democrats, sometimes we forget we're on the same team. When our battles become bigger and more important than the country, or the relationship itself, we stop focusing on what's really important."

"That's too true." She smiled ruefully. "How much better it would be if we were helping each other up instead of waiting for each other to fall down or fail. But how can *I* live by that rule when *he's* yelling at me or accusing me?"

"You're blinded by the fight. You can start by dropping your weapon."As soon as I said those words, a recollection stirred in my mind. "Jodi," I continued, "the words I just said triggered the memory of something I wrote down during the night last night. It's so pertinent to what we're talking about! Would you like to hear it?" She nodded.

> *There is no one fighting you. There never has been anyone fighting you. You don't enter into a relationship with the thought 'I'll make this other life miserable,' and neither does your partner. You both enter into the relationship because you see the gifts in each other. The appearance of attack is generated and maintained by you. It can only end when you stop fighting. If you don't relinquish your attacks entirely, you have not relinquished them at all.*

Your words are like magnets. Whatever you put out you attract back to you. Likewise, when another is firing from the opposite pole and it's not your fight, you can make the choice to drop your weapon and walk away and that energy will fly past you to attach elsewhere. Remember the only things that attach to you are the ones that you allow to attach.

You can only recognize in others what lives inside of yourself. Only attach to those belief systems that you want to attach to you. Allow all the rest to pass over you to find a different attachment. If someone is shooting at you and you shoot back, you have war. If someone is shooting at you and you step aside, he no longer has you to shoot at, and there will be no war. Your words are the same as weapons. They can be used for you or against you. It is your choice.

"That's powerful," Jodi said. "That means I can have more control of my life than I thought if I don't allow myself to get drawn back into the war."

"You've got it! You've got the option of just letting all his complaints and barbs fly right by you. If you get angry and fight back, you're both engaged in a losing battle."

Jodi said, "I always think that one day my real life will begin, when all these obstacles don't get in the way anymore."

BEING HAPPY RIGHT NOW

"Jodi, these obstacles *are* your life. There is no better time to be happy than right now. If not now, when? When your husband changes? When you get that new home? When your bills are finally paid off? We never know what the next moment will bring, or even if there will be a next moment. Don't postpone happiness. Time waits for no one. Treasure every moment.

"Instead of wishing for a fairy tale down the road, look at all the gifts hidden within you just waiting to be opened right now! Picture this. After you die and go to heaven, you're taken to a huge cathedral in the sky. Finally it's your turn to be face to face with God. In your moment of truth, you notice a huge pile of elaborately wrapped gifts, as high as you can see. You look over and ask, 'What is in all those packages?' God replies: 'Those are all the gifts I gave you on earth that you chose not to open.'

"How sad that I didn't open them," Jodi pondered. Then her eyes lit up like a child's at Christmas time. "But how wonderful that I have so many presents to open now! Which one should I open first?"

"You've already opened the presents of letting go of expectations and dropping your weapon. You told me you don't like it when John expects too much of you, correct?"

"Definitely."

"Then the next gift to open is giving you both room to breathe— the gift of shining by example. Stop telling each other what to do and not do. Nobody wants the 'how-to' approach these days. We're all burned out on being lectured to. How much more inspiring it would be if we could just mirror truth and happiness for each other! The way to do that is by taking the focus completely off of him, off of others, and put the focus on you, where it belongs."

TAKING CARE OF YOU FIRST

"Take care of you first. Take what you need for yourself."

"But that's against everything I was raised to believe!" she objected. "I was always taught to put others first, that it was selfish to think of yourself first."

"And look at the mess we've gotten ourselves into. We're a world full of people who are trying to fill everyone else up first while we're putting our own souls into a state of deprivation. The voice of our soul shrinks and fades into the background and we lose sight of who we are. Now we have a whole world of people listening to everyone on the outside for validation and not getting it, suffering from feelings of failure, and emotional and physical starvation. Take what you need for yourself. It is not an act of selfishness—it's an act of taking responsibility for yourself! It's an act of receiving the gift of love."

I could see her take a deep breath to make room for this new thought that honored her. "I never thought of it that way . . . It'll take getting used to, but it feels right somehow . . ."

"Of course it does. The place to start is with you. You've already said you don't know how to change John. And you can't! He doesn't want you to. So begin with what you *can* change—you. Relationship is about *allowing*, not trying to control or be controlled. Create the support you need within yourself. You're feeling neglected, so concentrate on you—making yourself happy. Don't expect anyone else to take on that job. As a bonus, you won't be disappointed in John anymore!"

Jodi's mind was opening to the possibilities of this new way of thinking. Her worried look gave way to a smile. "I'll bet John would even be relieved! It wouldn't be just a gift for myself—I'd be doing him a favor by getting off his back."

"You're so right. It would be such a favor to both of you. You'd both have room to breathe." For a moment, she slipped back into her old pattern. "It sounds so wonderful," she wailed, "but how on earth do I make myself happy when I've been feeling unhappy for so long? And anyway, aren't I supposed to be honoring all of my sad feelings?"

"You have been! That's all you've been doing. All you had were the sad thoughts. Trust me, you've got the sadness mastered." She grinned and nodded. "You're right. I'm ready to move out of that."

TURNING IT AROUND: HIGHLIGHTING THE GOOD

"Another gift you can open right now is learning how to refocus away from that sadness and away from your former battles. Stop looking at everything that's wrong. John isn't going to change. The world isn't going to change. You can't change them. What you can change is how you look at them! Look with more flexible eyes. Here's a simple technique that will produce immediate results. You'll be amazed.

"Here's how it works. Jodi, sit up for a moment. I want you to look around this room and find everything that's red." She looked intently for all the red objects within the room. "Now close your eyes," I directed her. She did. "Now I want you to tell me everything that is green." She couldn't. She hadn't "seen" one green object. She understood what I was getting at. Whatever she was focusing on became her reality, even though it wasn't the "real" picture of the entire room. She "saw" only the red, just as she was "seeing" only the "bad" things in her marriage.

"This is how to see through fresh eyes: Focus on the good things in your marriage. By always focusing on what you're not getting out of the relationship, the problems and the voids only grow deeper. No wonder you were feeling so drained and depleted! When we focus on everything that we aren't doing right, we become paranoid, paralyzed with fear of rejection, of being criticized, of being wrong or not pleasing. Focus on what's good instead! It's much more fun."

There was a glimmer of relief in her eyes. She said, "I feel as if you're helping me climb out of a deep hole that I've dug for myself."

"Good. Tell me what you first loved about John and what is positive about your life together."

Her face brightened. "I fell in love with his wonderful heart and spirit. He was a great guy, handsome, affectionate, playful and talented! He's a good provider, and we have a nice home. We adore our little one-year-old daughter and are healthy and could have another child even though we're in our forties . . ." Her whole body reflected the relaxing influence of good thoughts feeding her soul. She sat up straighter, and her face glowed.

"That's wonderful. Now you're recapturing your original vision of you two together—your intentions were so good: to have a happy life with this wonderful man."

"I'd love to hold onto that—but without the expectations this time. How do I do that?"

"Good for you! Now you're learning. You know, I only select people to work with who are into action. Better not come to me unless you're ready to change and move fast! And you are. And so is John. This is exciting." She beamed.

"Now, as to how to let go of expectations and honor each other, perhaps this visualization, this little parable, will help."

THE ROYAL PLATTER

I asked her to place her left hand out, palm up. "See yourself with a large platter in your hand. Imagine that you are a Queen in a banquet hall. There is a sumptuous smorgasbord to choose from. This gathering is a very special occasion—your life! The waiters are walking around holding their silver platters, making offerings to you. "Would you like to try this, Your Majesty?" they ask. You either accept or graciously decline the offerings. Choice by choice, you fill your royal plate.

"Without hesitation you turn to your friends and say, 'You should really try this. It's delicious!' Suddenly, in your eyes, you see them—and even the waiters—not as subjects, but as worthy equals, turned into kings and queens themselves. You serve them your delicious offerings. They in turn make offerings to each other. All these generous royal people are holding out their serving platters for the whole room, making mutual offerings.

"Everyone is making their own choices as to what they want to add to their plate. Each has the option to say, *No thank you, I don't believe I want that one,* always being gracious, saying *Thank you for asking.* Everyone's words, suggestions and choices are offered and viewed as valuable. Everyone is deciding whether they want to put something on their plate, ingest it immediately, save it until later or completely reject it. Whatever choices they make are the right ones for them, and they're content because everyone else in the room is happy for them—because everyone else is also happy with their own selections.

"Now I want you to become aware of who's serving you. Some servers will look more appealing to you, some offerings will seem more valuable. And you must also become aware of what you are offering in return and whom you're offering it to.

"In our lives, as in this make-believe banquet, when we are approached with a suggestion or a demand, we must view it simply as an offering. We must hold out our platter and then ask ourselves, *Does this serve me or not?* If we think that it *does* serve us, we taste it, try it on, and if it feels good and our spirit opens up and our gut feelings like it, we accept it and internalize it. If, on the other hand, it makes us constrict and feel tight, all we have to do is say, *Thank you, that doesn't serve me,* and decline the offer. We do not need to justify our choice to anyone, but simply take it or leave it. Life will never stop offering. The difference now is that we know we are in choice regarding what we want to take in."

"I'm entranced. That simplifies things. Now let's see if I can apply the royal platter technique to one of my pet peeves."

EVERYDAY OFFERINGS AND CHOICES

"On the weekends, I want John to go on a walk with me and the baby, but he just plops down on the couch and takes a nap instead. If he loves me, how can he just sleep away what little time he has away from work and not be with me and the baby? That's totally selfish! Oops! There I go. Past thinking, right?"

"Yup, you slipped back in there for a moment. Your idea of love is that he gives up his need to rest to take a walk with you. His idea of love is that you give up your need for him to walk with you and let him rest ."

"That's where I'm getting stuck—thinking he has to do what I want him to, or being afraid I'll have to give up what I want to please him or love him. But . . . if we can each choose what we want off the royal platter, then I could offer him the appetizer of a walk. If he chooses not to take it and take the dessert of a nap instead, I could go on my walk anyway . . . and still be mad as heck because he's not with me!" It was good to see her laughing at herself. "That'll be the tough part—not getting angry."

"It always is. We've got to let go of that outcome. But you're well on your way! Maybe next time, because you've given him the space to make up his own mind, he'll be inspired to join in the fun with you. But don't count on it, and that will free you to enjoy yourself with or without him."

"This is getting to be fun. What's next, coach?"

"Now we get to the heart of the whole matter. Honoring yourself first and honoring others at the same time by allowing them to be who they are. A very courageous step. I shared some more:

IT IS YOUR COLLECTIVE DIFFERENCES THAT CREATE THE MAGNIFICENT WHOLE

You attract all relationships into your life to
complement and expand your own personal growth.
Relationship is about creating a feeling inside
and with others that helps you create a more loving and
more powerful existence.
As my partner, you stand as an original!
One of a kind, you will shine upon the world.
I support every step that you take.
Trust and allow for yourself and always allow for others.
The brilliant differences of each individual
will collectively create the Whole.
I have imprinted an everlasting impression
upon your fingertips—your fingerprints—
to remind you that no two are intended to be alike
and to remind you that there is never
only one way of doing things.

Jodi looked at her own fingerprints. "Nobody in the whole world has my prints. I am one-of-a-kind—unique! And so is John. I tend to forget that, though, when we're trying to figure out who we are as a couple."

A WORLD OF RELATIONSHIPS IN YOUR OWN BODY

"That's the challenge for all of us—how to be in a relationship with yourself first and then with others. Our own body can provide a map. Within you lives an inner world that is in constant relationship with you. Every organ in your body has an individual and unique contribution. The purpose of your heart is to pump blood; the purpose of your liver is to detoxify; the purpose of your pancreas is to produce insulin.

All your organs are connected and powered by the same energy—*innate intelligence.* Picture the varied organs in your body as being like the varied people on the planet. We are all connected to the same energy, keeping us alive, yet we can only see through our own eyes. If your heart were a person, it might think, *Why isn't everyone pumping blood?* Your liver's belief system might be that everyone should detoxify. The pancreas might think every other organ is without question doing the wrong thing, for not one of them is producing insulin. Each organ may never understand what the other is doing, yet they live in the same land and contribute individually to the whole. If each one does its own part, trusting all the others to hold up their end, balance is created. They all trust in innate intelligence to coordinate the individual efforts and they all work together for the magnificent operation of your body as a whole!"

Jodi was radiant with this new consciousness. "Amazing! So by just being who I am all by myself—by taking what I need and doing my job for me, I *am* contributing to the whole! So I'm *not* being selfish by taking for me, after all. How liberating!"

"You're so right. It's the opposite of being selfish. The whole world benefits when you take responsibility for your own life. That means everyone else can be free to take care of themselves, not having to worry about you for the most part. They'll be glad to pitch in and help and support you when you need it, but they won't be constantly thrown off balance trying to do your job for you. Everyone benefits when you make sure you are happy."

We were both so excited by this profound awareness that the energy in the room felt infinite. We talked excitedly about the implications of what we were working out together. These truths and techniques weren't only for husbands and wives—they could be applied to everyone in every situation in all relationships! Brothers and sisters, boyfriends and girlfriends, partners in businesses, co-workers in organizations, even state to state and nation to nation. Honoring and celebrating our differences while allowing for each other, which creates a more beautiful Whole.

BLENDERS AND TOASTERS

You could really see the wheels turning in Jodi's mind. "You know, before I was always so discouraged, thinking about how John and I were so different—how we never saw eye to eye. We were literally trying to force each other to see things our own way! No wonder we were so stuck. And we weren't wrong to resist being coerced."

I picked up on this thread: " . . . because deep inside you knew you should honor the way you feel. People don't have to agree, support or convince. They simply must *allow*. Convincing people to take actions that is not in alignment with their souls or lessons at that time, will only create separation. If we feel like giving advice, maybe we had better listen closely and take that advice ourselves. People don't listen to unsolicited advice anyway. They hear only the implied criticism.

"People aren't meant to see eye to eye! We don't even have to agree with each other. We can give up trying to convince everyone to see it our way. What a breath of fresh air. All we have to do is ALLOW! Allow for the differences, honor them. Allow for the other opinion. Listen. Allow for the feelings of others. Don't try to change them."

She added, understanding: "And that could free us to come to better conclusions together because we trust . . ."

". . . and we've let go of the expectations and the outcome. Beautiful. Jodi, I know you're not going to want to try to 'fix' John anymore because now you understand that he isn't 'broken.' We aren't a world full of broken people. We're just all learning our lessons! There's even a good reason why we get so stuck on seeing what's wrong in others—those are the things we want to change in ourselves!"

"So if I get the urge to fix John, I'll just fix myself instead! But it's going to take lots of practice to retrain myself out of my old ways of being and reacting."

"That's exactly what I was thinking, and a picture popped into my mind. If a time comes when you are tempted to 'fix' John instead of yourself, think of this: in the kitchen, we have all different kinds of appliances, each with its own purpose. They're all plugged into the same electrical source, just like we're all connected to the same energy source. They all do their own jobs. A toaster is supposed to toast— that's its purpose in life; a blender is supposed to blend, that's *its* purpose in life. We only see through the eyes of who we are. So if you're a toaster, through *your* eyes, everyone should toast. If our spouse is a blender, he's thinking everybody should blend. Simply respect and allow for differences."

"I get it," she said. "All the time I've been attempting the hopeless task of trying to turn John into a toaster, when he was a blender all along. It will be easier now to see and appreciate what he does well— how he sees his job and purpose. The beauty of this is, I don't have to try to be like anybody else anymore—in fact, it's better if I don't! Boy, have I had that backwards.. There's something that still worries me, though. I'm really ready to make these changes. What if John doesn't like the new me? And what if he doesn't want to change?"

HOLDING PATTERNS

"We need to expand when we are ready, so we can grow at our own rate and model growth for others. They'll take a look at what you're doing and take action when they're ready. People are sometimes afraid their spouses don't want them to grow, but that's usually not the case. They're usually just afraid their spouse will try to change *them!* If you leave them alone and allow them to be who they are and don't criticize, no problem. You can become a shining light that inspires them to want the same happiness. They may have to stay in a holding pattern—where they are at that moment—until they figure things out. Look at how long it took you before you wanted to change! But you've made that decision. And look how fast you're growing now! So just *allow* for John's holding patterns.

Here's another story to help with this final process. Trust that others can do it too. I want you to take a deep breath . . .

Ready . . .

Let . . .

Go . . . of all expectations.

THE STORY OF THE TWO FLOWER BULBS

"Everyone is a flower in the garden of life, growing at his or her own pace. Close your eyes and follow along with me. Visualize a beautiful green garden to your right side. There's an empty patch of land covered with topsoil. Go over to that land and dig a nice deep hole in the earth. Take these two flower bulbs that potentially will be blooms and plant them one on top of the other. Now cover your hole and water your bulbs. Watch them grow. Visualize the bulb on the bottom. Its roots can grow deep and strong but it must grow around the top bulb to reach the surface of the ground. Its strength and determination might be so strong it can push the top bulb out of the ground as it stretches and reaches for its light source—not meaning to harm the top bulb, but just doing its job trying to survive and thrive. It can't just grow straight up to connect to its light source. It must take a detour.

"Now visualize the top bulb. It can grow straight up, but its roots must take a detour as well. It must grow around the bottom bulb and might even, without realizing it, smother or strangle the bottom bulb, just trying to survive, trying to connect with its light source, to ground its roots in the earth. Neither the top nor the bottom bulb can win in this situation.

"Now visualize another empty patch of land covered with topsoil. This time plant your flower bulbs two feet apart and watch them grow. They each have room for their roots to spread (at their own rate, space and time) and room to blossom into beautiful flowers as they each reach out of the earth toward the common light source of energy. As your bulbs grow, see that when given their own space, they grow and blossom into a beautiful garden, complementing each other, but not intruding upon one another. That's where the balance lies. The magnificence of the garden as a whole developed from each separate energy blossoming at its own time and rate and growing within its own path."

Jodi beamed with understanding. Her whole body was relaxed now. "I truly wasn't trying to strangle John. I can't wait to get home and tell him. My back even feels better.

"Remember how he really was trying when he left here? I think he wants to change and work this out, too." Tears came to her eyes. "How can this be? An hour ago I wanted to leave my husband. In this moment, I am beginning to feel again as if I'm the luckiest woman alive!"

Jodi left in a euphoric state of mind, having replaced all her negative thoughts with positive ones—for the moment anyway. A very fine start. Maybe she and John would meet on some level in their combined euphoria. The king and queen were about to reunite. As for me, I couldn't wait to rejoin my own royal family. However . . .

I was in for a surprise myself.

The Gift
of Knowing

The seed of knowledge is hidden;

your task is to make it known.

As your mind and soul develop,

you will look deeper into the same

words to find different meanings,

thus creating fresh actions

and new experiences.

You will achieve great success

when you master the universal

language of intention

behind the words.

There is a Hidden Language Behind the Words

Rushing into my house, I was eager to share with my husband the latest insights of my week's experiences. My mind couldn't switch tracks. It felt like I was on receive-and-send automatic pilot. I ran up to him and said breathlessly, "Danny, guess what? You'll never believe the incredible breakthroughs Jodi has had in her healing! She really understands how she's been expecting too much and . . ." He interrupted, "Jill, wait! This is going to have to stop. You are way out of balance."

His words sounded so harsh. I felt as if cold water had been poured over me. My mind shifted into a defensive mode—a protection mentality—and made me want to fight back. Before I could launch a counter-barrage, his next words revealed his true intention.

"Sweetheart, I'm worried. Look at you—your face is drawn and strained; your eyes are glazed over from not sleeping. You've been running on sheer adrenaline all week. You must be on overload, keeping up with your heavy patient schedule on top of all this other stuff. It's not healthy. Can you cancel appointments today or tomorrow and take some time off? You need rest big time, maybe, to start with, a hot bath . . ."

My first perception had been that he was angry with me, but it turned out that he was really concerned about me. I melted into his warm hug. I thought, *How lucky I am to have a man who can express his feelings so well. What if he had stopped with the first couple of sentences? Then I might have countered emotionally and we would have had a fight in no time.* Knowing his intention made my response easier.

"Danny, " I said, "thank you for thinking of me, but I feel this is a gift. I trust deep down that when it's ready to end, it will." He replied, "What if this goes on for years? What if it never ends? What about me? What about the kids? We want time with you, too."

"I know." I hugged him. "Please allow me this for now. I choose to stay in my process." He said, "If this is what you think is best for you, I support you. I'm only trying to help."

ENDLESS NIGHTS

How long this process would last was a mystery to us all. Danny's words did help pull me back into my life. I, too, was craving time with my family. That evening I spent time with Danny and we read and played with our children. By nine o'clock, the children were tucked in bed and fast asleep, and I had slowed down.

"Let's go to bed," Danny suggested. I remembered my previous nights of fruitless attempts at sleep and said, "Optimistic, aren't we!" but I followed him upstairs, hoping. I felt more balanced and relaxed than I had for a few days.

The night was beautiful and cool. Just as I was getting comfortable and ready to rest, Danny opened our bedroom window. I actually felt scared for a moment and said, "Maybe you'd better shut it. I don't know whether I can take it if these messages come through any faster!" We laughed. I chose to keep the window open for I knew, deep down, that *the more I can take, the more I will become.*

CONTRIBUTION

Lying in bed, however, I began questioning. *Was Danny right? Was I getting too absorbed and out of balance? Was I doing the right thing? On the other hand, by being in this process, wasn't I making a contribution to our family? As my children witnessed my beautiful experience, wasn't I showing them that we have the capability to understand and interpret spirit in our daily lives?* Maybe because I wasn't only "mommy" for a few days, the children perceived I didn't have time for them. But I knew deep down it was O.K. to take this time. My intention—my experience—would help us all. I recognized that I was going through a form of transition. My mind and soul were growing rapidly.

People change constantly—their jobs, their hair, their possessions, their relationships. Every role in life is under constant construction. I kept asking myself, *Aren't we still all contributors, even as we're going through these transitions? Is it our age, our position, our role in life that determines our level of contribution?* Maybe our contribution is relevant to our capacity at that time.

As I continued to think, I drifted in and out. Like waves in the sea, my spirit—and the process—started flowing. I began writing once more:

> *Hold on tight, then let go. Embrace your intention, but never stay attached to an outcome, for your gift may be revealed in unexpected ways. Remain fluid and flexible along your journey; you are being prepared to listen deeper. You are entering into a new state of learning.*

*Energy will always rise to the highest level of
thought. The moment an advanced thought is achieved
in our universe, the awareness spreads, and it becomes
available for all. You are part of a collective consciousness. As you replenish yourself to broaden as an individual, you are creating an opening to contribute to all.
We as one create our expanded realities!*

I felt as if I were in a deep conversation. Questions flew through my
mind. The energy in the room moved faster. I had so many thoughts,
so many questions. My soul craved answers. I asked, *Are all of our contributions equal?* I didn't have to wait long for an answer . . .

*ALL CONTRIBUTIONS ARE VALUABLE:
Regardless of your age or level of intelligence, all
contributions are valuable. The quality of your thoughts
reflects the quality of your life. Life is a trust game of
taking, replenishing, and building on the undisclosed;
for what lies in every moment is unidentified. Your
power comes from the lessons learned by challenging
those moments, turning thought processes into achievement. As you continually take to fill yourself up, you
grow and learn and overflow your truth and abundance
to create your balance. By your example, you allow others to take and add to their experience.*

*No matter who or where you are in life, the here and
now is your only time. The universe measures your level
of contribution not by how far you have progressed intel-
lectually but by how willing you are to grow from the
level where you are right now. You are all created equal.*

I had to challenge that thought. *Is my contribution equally as valuable
as Albert Einstein's?* My thoughts traveled deeper still and I listened at
an infinite level:

EVERYONE'S AN EINSTEIN

Whenever you expand and grow, you are participating in the growth of the entire universe. You are here to master each of your lessons, regardless of the task. Once you have learned a lesson, the universe expands and says, "Thank you!"

Does it matter if you're Albert Einstein or a brand new baby?

A vision of a young baby appeared in my mind. The baby was struggling, trying to figure out how to roll over. Repeatedly it tried, challenging itself constantly. At last, the baby mastered it—it succeeded, and I saw its mind stretch and its soul grow and I saw it say thank you. At the same time, the heavens opened up a bit wider and bowed down to the baby with gratitude for its contribution. In the same way, in order to stretch to his next level of thought, Albert Einstein's mind obviously needed to figure out the theory of relativity for his soul to grow and say thank you. As a result, our universe expanded in grace and honor. We all must constantly strive for the next step at our own level. Whether you are a new baby or you're Albert Einstein, you are making the same contributions in life. We all go up together!

Maybe that's what this week has been about, I thought—a balancing act between my spirit and mind to challenge me to another level. We are all adding experiences to our lives to enhance our stories. Yes, I saw it clearly. Our stories grow, and we grow along with them. The secret that so many of us forget is that we can write the story ourselves, and it's our own script to follow.

When we are writing our script, however, it is obvious to me through working with my patients that our story usually falls apart around the words. Breakdown of communication is the ultimate cause of separation. I wondered why.

The seed of knowledge is hidden; your task is to make it known. As your mind and soul develop, you will look deeper into the same words to find different meanings, thus creating fresh actions and new experiences. You will achieve great success when you master the universal language of intention behind the words.

That's it! The "universal language of intention behind the words." That must be the key to the whole problem of breakdown in communication! It was all coming together. I thought back to one of my patients and how words were creating separation instead of closeness between a mother and son.

LEAVE ME ALONE!

Michael is a nice young man raised in a traditional family. All his life it was drilled into his head: "You should grow up to become a doctor or a lawyer!" Michael ended up becoming a *clown!* Not just an ordinary clown, but a clown who helps children who have cancer. Michael loved his career and felt very fulfilled. However, his mother didn't feel the same way. Every other day she'd call Michael.

"Michael are you still doing that clown thing? When are you going to get a real job? Are you still living in that little apartment? Don't you have a girlfriend yet? You really should think about getting married and buying a home and making a life for yourself."

Michael would shout back, "Mom, leave me alone! If I want to be a clown, I'm going to be a clown! If I want to live in an apartment, I'll live in an apartment. Stop telling me what I should or shouldn't do. It's my life! If you're going to keep criticizing me, just don't call at all!" He'd always hang up angry.

"Michael," I asked, "during your conversations with your mom, were you creating closeness or separation?"

"Sometimes I can't even stand being in the same room with her," he said. "She sets me off constantly. Why can't she either love me for myself or just leave me alone?"

"What if this is the only way she knows how to show love?"

"If that's what love feels like, I'd rather not have it!" he exclaimed.

"Michael, your mother's words can only come through the eyes of who she is. Your mother has been trained to see success in a certain way. Maybe she's trying to say 'I love you' in the only way she knows how. She's not trying to control your life; she wants the best for you. Her comments show you what she sees as being the best. Her intention isn't to create separation from you. Your mother loves you. Maybe in her eyes being a doctor and living in a big house with wife and kids is how she views happiness and success.

"When she talks to you next time, I suggest that you listen only to her *intentions* and bypass her words. Forget the words and hear her saying, 'I care about you, I want so much for you, my son, I love you.' Let's see what happens. Remember, only speak to her intentions. She is saying 'I love you' the best way she can."

"It'll never work," he declared. "She'll never change." But he reluctantly agreed to try.

A few days later Michael's mom phoned him and started her speech. "Michael, when are you going to get a real job, get married, buy a house and have children?"

Michael paused and answered, "Mom, thank you for wanting so much for me."

Instantly, his mother broke down and sobbed, "That's all I've ever been trying to say! I love you, Son."

THE HIDDEN LANGUAGE

As Michael discovered, life is much easier if we learn to understand the motivation behind the words. Maybe we get into trouble when we take words at face value. If only we can open up to what people are really trying to say, we will avoid much pain.

It was two o'clock in the morning. Still wide awake, I went into the kitchen and packed the kids' lunches and got their backpacks ready for school. As I loaded their books, one by one, I thought, here we are, learning languages like French, Spanish and English. We go to class, we listen to teachers, we take tests, we're graded. We learn to excel because we want to get it right. Then, after all that training, we get out into the world and no one understands what the other person is trying to say! Even when we're speaking in the same language! What's going on? Why this breakdown of communication? Why are people fighting to be heard? Why is it so difficult to figure out what the other person is trying to say?

HOME-SCHOOLED IN THE
LANGUAGE OF EMOTIONS

The light went on in my head. I had figured out another mystery. We have difficulty understanding each other because we are *home-schooled* in the *language of emotions.* We all learn the same "language" and we use the same words, but every one of us attaches different emotions and perceptions to the same words according to our past experiences around those words, initially in our "school" at home. Consequently, we may be using the same words, but in reality, we're speaking different languages.

FLYING WORDS AND ANTENNA-FILTERS

Scene after scene popped into my head, in location after location, of human beings trying to communicate with each other. They all had little antennae on top of their heads. I watched the words whizzing back and forth on the airwaves between them from mouth (message sent) to antenna (message received). The problems seemed to happen during the "flight."

In flight, the words swirled around like tornados!

Words go up... Words come down
Words get los t....

Words get jumbled

Words swirl around like tornados! Tornados! Tornados! Tornados! Tornados!

They got mixed up with

emotions   history   family conditioning   gender
mood that day   physical condition   environment
time available   influence of others   preceding events

A few made it through to the receiver.

Messages were processed in an instant

through antennae filters according to individual truths.

Receiver's *interpretation*—usually different from the sender's.

HUSBAND
Honey, I'm going to play golf
with the guys this weekend.
Intention: (Boy, I've been working hard! I sure deserve this!)

WIFE
Perception: (He doesn't love me, or he'd want to be with me.)
You said you'd spend time with me
and the kids!

BREAKDOWN!

BOSS
Janice, can you get this stack of
letters out by noon?
Intention: (It's sure great to have a super secretary to help me get this done on time!)

SECRETARY
Perception: (Who does he think I am? Super Woman? No way!)
Sure, boss.

BREAKDOWN!

GIRLFRIEND
Want to go to dinner Friday
night?
Intention: (Romance! La Parisienne, flowers, candlelight, music.)

BOYFRIEND
Perception: (Man, the Braves game's Friday night.)
Sure! Let's catch a hamburger and
the game at Taco Mac.

BREAKDOWN!

DAUGHTER
Hi, Mom, how are ya doing?
Intention: (Haven't spoken to Mom in a while, I'll give her a call.)

MOTHER
Perception: (My kids have forgotten me.)
What, you don't have any time for
me anymore?

BREAKDOWN!

FATHER
```
Son, how 'bout we work on that
hot rod you're building this
weekend.
```
Intention: (I want to spend more time with my son.)

SON
Perception: (The old man's never going to have confidence in me!)
```
Geez, Dad, don't you think I can
do anything by myself?
```

BREAKDOWN!

Getting Past the Words

In order to understand each other, we must *learn to look past words and our emotional attachments to them, decipher the underlying motivations behind words,* and *respond to the intention, not to the words themselves.* We can stop creating communication breakdowns if we go beyond the words and keep an open mind.

So often, for example, when patients with serious illnesses hear a doctor say, "I'm sorry we don't have the answers; there's nothing more we can do," they get paralyzed with fear. They literally let those words stop them. They think, *I'm doomed.* What they can learn to do is keep an open mind and get beyond the words. *O.K., if he doesn't have the answers, who does? If that doctor isn't the catalyst, who or what is? Where else do I go to find my answers?* Everybody's middle name should be "Flexible." Life isn't going to change. Language isn't going to change. But we can change the way we hear it and interpret it.

Sometimes we take offense when we're trying to protect our own point of view. If intention is not the primary focus as the words fly back and forth, all too often we want to "kill the messenger," viewing him or her as the opposition.

When I had been receiving these messages, I had asked the question, *If we're all equally valuable, why is there so much competition? Why does each of us believe our way is the right way? Why do we insist upon proving and protecting our old ways to the bitter end? Why are we so attached to our own words?* The answers had shouted out in my mind:

THE NEED TO BE RIGHT

Everyone wants to be right. The need to be right is a camouflage to create validation—to feel honored and approved of, even if prematurely. A society that looks for approval more than it looks for lessons in life will become filled with deprivation. If you focus on the lessons, you will rise up out of the endless repetition of unsatisfying results.

LISTEN WITH FLEXIBLE EARS

We are here to gather information from each other and to seek deeper truths within ourselves. The learning comes from listening. I have left you with another lasting impression to help you remember to listen—ears with flexible cartilage so they stand out from your head—to encourage you to listen well and remain in a state of curiosity. All offerings are valuable, most especially the ones you do not wish to hear! As you gather information, you will be able to determine whether there is a deeper truth within that perhaps you do not yet recognize. This will be your clue: you will only react to protect yourself if what is said does in fact live within you.

My mind created another scenario:

GREEN HAIR?

Someone approached me and said, "Wow, your green hair looks great today!" I started laughing. "Are you crazy?" I replied. "My hair is brown." His words didn't bother me at all because I knew without a doubt that I do not have green hair.

Then a different picture flashed in my mind. I was born with green hair and had been taught my whole life to cover it up and color my hair brown. *Always make sure the green never shows through,* I was warned.

Now when the same words were directed towards me, I was offended and went into protective mode. "Green hair? You're crazy, I don't have green hair!" This time his words bothered me, because I knew there was a deeper truth that lived within me that I was indeed denying and trying to cover up.

IN LEARNING OR IN PROTECTION?

Words are a form of energy.
There are only two directions in which this energy
can travel—toward you or away from you.
Energy expands or contracts.
Expanding energy is the energy of learning.
It comes from choice and desire—an open energy.
Contracting energy results from resistance.
This energy comes from a place of need or obligation.
This is the energy of protection—a closed energy—
an energy to redirect.

Your perceptions and interpretations of your communi-
cations will create an expanding experience or a con-

tracting one. Being in a state of learning will always
expand energy. Being in a state of protection will always
contract energy. When someone makes an observation or
offers a suggestion that you find difficult to take in, you
may find yourself going into a protective mode and con-
fronting the person. When this happens, your energy
will contract and you will resist learning. Another form
of contracting energy is blaming others or proving them
wrong. When you respond in a judgmental way, your
energy is closed and resistant to learning.

People do not have to agree, support, or persuade.
They simply must allow. By persuading another to take
an action that is not in alignment with their soul at
that time, you will create separation.

Come from curiosity and ask why? Once you have
ownership to your truth, then the opinions of others will
not affect you, merely becoming information for your
growth. When you are in ownership of self (worth) then
everyone who comes into your life emerges as valuable
in some way. All judgment will be dropped. Your eyes
will stop seeing the faults in others and look for like
minds to reflect greatness as they reflect your beliefs of
self. When you feel resistance, you can see it positively
as a sign that you are about to be redirected into an
unfamiliar, but potentially valuable, lesson. It may also
be an opportunity to clarify your own intent and new
reality.

Because of the newness of my words to her ears, I had one new
patient who almost didn't come back to see me. She was suffering
from a variety of ailments and had been through all the medical
treatments available with no relief. I clearly remember our first
session. As I launched into my passionate discussion of advanced

theories on healing, I could see her mind stretch, yet she remained reserved and cautious. The next time I saw her, she told me, "Dr. Jill, I almost didn't come back." "You didn't?" I questioned. "Why is that?"

She said, "Your way of thinking and speaking is so different from mine. It's like nothing I have ever heard—it's like a different language."

I teased, "Your way is what got you into this mess. You might want to consider hearing something that's a little different!" She smiled and nodded.

As time went on, she become familiar with my language and stretched into a new state of learning. She gained a knowingness in her ability to heal. She always referred to me as her "feel-good doctor." The truth is, I don't only make people feel good. They feel good because they heal themselves on the inside. After each session, she would turn to me and say, "I like the way you think!"

Another time, the tables were turned on me—I wasn't comfortable with the words flying at me from my husband. I was just learning the power of clarifying my intentions in language. My friend Elisa had dropped in for a visit.

OLD TAPES/NEW SONGS

Elisa couldn't wait to tell me her news: "I'm thinking about opening up a beauty salon!" She wanted my opinion, which I was delighted to provide. I knew all about that business, since my parents had owned and operated beauty salons my entire life. As we finished our brainstorming, Danny called down and said, "Hey, Elisa, come up and hear my new song!" The two of us zoomed upstairs. Elisa, so keyed up, told Danny how much I had helped her and that I had given her many creative ideas about her project! Danny glanced over at me then back at Elisa and said, "That Jill—can't she ever let people figure things out by themselves?"

Now I could have taken offense and retaliated, and maybe in the old days I would have. Instead, I got beyond those words and the old sensitivities. I chose to bounce it back the way I felt it. I said, "That's funny, I thought how fortunate I was to have had the time and experience to help my friend." Elisa agreed. Danny responded gracefully, "You know, you're right. Let me know how it turns out." Danny played his song.

This is what I registered in my heart: *I am useful.* My mind's "tape" recorded: *My husband understands me.* I must only record messages according to how I want to interpret them *myself,* not from the words that are projected by someone else.

A CINDERELLA STORY OF COMMUNICATION: BETH AND RICKY'S STORY

Still awake in the wee hours of the morning, I was going through my e-mails and took joy in re-reading an old one from Beth, one of my patients. Her experience is an incredible story of learning how to break out of unsuccessful communication patterns.

Beth was referred to me when she was at the lowest of the lows. She had just split up with Ricky, the man she loved. Ricky had been divorced twice because he absolutely could not express his feelings. His worst fear was breaking up with someone. He was so petrified that a woman would go away if he said what he felt that his verbal equipment was paralyzed—which turned out to be the reason women left him! He drew his worst fear to himself.

Even though Ricky loved Beth very much, he was unable to communicate with her—afraid, as he been in other relationships, that if he said what he really felt, she'd leave him. Her biggest complaint about him was when she told him how *she* felt, he brushed her off and said everything was O.K.—either that or he tried to "fix" her. When she'd say she wanted to talk some more about a matter, he'd counter, "I gave you three solutions and you haven't acted on them, so what do you want from me?" She really just wanted to be heard. Obviously, that was never going to happen, so she split up with him. It was terrible for Ricky—yet another woman he loved had left him. He felt like a failure and became very resentful. If Beth called to talk, he'd just say "Get out of my life!"

When Beth first came to me, she was in terrible shape. All she could talk about was Ricky and how she was the victim. I urged her to take her focus off him and taking what she needed by refocusing on herself. She blossomed. She learned her own worth and made up her mind not to settle for anything less than what she wanted!

I asked Beth, "What do you want in a man?" She gave me a long list that included things like "generous, outdoorsy, loves children, loves to go on vacations, listens to me, and knows how to express his feelings."

I said, "The person you are describing is *you*. That's what you want in a man—a reflection of what you are and what you love." It was amazing. Once she realized what she really wanted, she started meeting all kinds of men who fit her description exactly! They wined and dined Beth, the Queen. One guy absolutely adored her—bought her diamonds and took her to exotic vacation spots.

One day she happened to run into Ricky. He saw the confidence in her and loved it. He said, "Whatever you did, I want it!" She told him how I had helped her, and he wanted to see me, too. She called me and said, "My ex-boyfriend wants to come to you and I'd like for him to see you, but maybe it's not in my best interest for him to come to the same person."

I said, "That depends upon what *your* interest is. If your interest is to see he grows as you have, then send him." So she did, and he worked on changing himself, too, while she continued to date the other man who loved her.

Beth asked me how Ricky was doing. She wanted to know why he could tell *me* how he feels and not her? I said, "Men—and women, too—want to be heard and listened to, not criticized. He feels safe with me. I don't go home with him, I'm not his patrol, making sure he's following through with what he said he would do. We don't want a parent or baby sitter, we want a lover, a mate, a friend!"

I kept coaching both of them to stop focusing on the other person. I reassured Ricky that resistance he felt from a woman wasn't about him, but was about where she was at the moment with herself. I kept encouraging them, *Concentrate on what you want, and then just allow for the other person.* Ricky is a much more relaxed person than Beth. He enjoys putting his feet up and watching TV. Beth has a very active lifestyle and is a professional fast-walker. When they were in a relationship, she feared losing her freedom. I told her, "You don't have to have the same lives. He supports your lifestyle, so don't try to change his. Simply allow."

I coached them separately in developing their listening skills: "If someone says something you don't agree with, don't close up and say, 'You're wrong!' Try instead, 'Please tell me more about your viewpoint,' and examine their point of view for what may be useful to you. It's still your choice. You can digest it or discard it. Ask the other person, 'What are you trying to tell me?' Then try very hard to *listen.* Don't let the words trigger you into your old insecurities and modes of protection."

Somewhere in the middle of their healing process, Ricky asked Beth out to dinner and they started dating again. They were engrossed in each other's lessons and shared one of their frequent e-mails with me. Obviously, Ricky was learning his lesson about how to communicate!

ONE LESSON LEARNED, ONE SCRIPT THAT WORKED

```
Dear Bethie,
   Can I come over tonight?
I love you—Ricky
```

• • •

```
Dear Ricky,
   I would love it if you came over, but lately I
have had a lot on my mind. There's a part of me
that would love for you to pop over regardless
of how I feel, but I really need time for me
now. I feel so connected to you and I hope you
understand what I am trying to say. Please
understand it isn't anything you've done. It's
about me and my feelings. My needs are important
to me as well as pleasing you and us. It's that
communication and understanding that is so
important. I do understand your wants and
desires for us to be together. I still get
caught within myself just trying to do the right
thing. I would like it if you would pose some
options. At least I would feel you are with me
and recognize my own needs as well. Plus, this
time of year always affects me, since it's the
anniversary of my mother's death. I know subcon-
sciously it's weighing on me. So, I guess Ricky,
I have a lot going on.
   I love you honey—Beth
```

• • •

```
Dear Bethie,
   Honey, I got your email, read it a couple of
times—just to make sure I understood.
```

We can talk more on the phone tonight if it would help, but in the meantime just know that I do understand what you need to do for yourself. When you take care of yourself, our relationship is stronger as well, so I want you to keep focusing on it.

What I hear you saying is that you want me to be particularly sensitive to your needs during this time. I am also aware of how tough it is sometimes to juggle "us" when you have a lot going on. You also know that I'm working on myself to learn to give you the time that you need for yourself and to be aware of not putting pressure on you. I am determined to do just that. If I should occasionally fail at this, it would mean a lot to me if you could just give me a loving reminder and I promise to make it happen.

The communication we've had recently has been so refreshing and loving that I want us to keep it up. It has become easy for me to share my thoughts with you, but your feedback and reminders are so important for me while I am learning to make it a regular part of our relationship. I don't want to slip back into any old habits.

So, I will promise to always keep you and your needs as a priority. You will have all of my support, communication and love for as long as you want it—not just during this time. Just be careful not to depend on me to always know what you need at the exact time that you need it. I can do this a lot, but I am not perfect and I love having you continue to tell me your needs. That may not always be the most romantic way to get what you need, but it sure has been a noticeable and wonderful change that I have seen in you recently. And it has made me feel so much more open with you because I don't have to worry if my crystal ball gets cloudy some days.

I really do love you deeply, Bethie, and I am totally committed to keeping you the number one priority in my life. What we have is stronger now than it ever was before, and I really like the softness, forgiveness and tenderness that we give to each other. The past is history. It gives us a wonderful foundation to build on and a relationship that has become richer through

```
both the good and the not so good experiences.
    Please let me know if I have heard you cor-
rectly and if this note is on target. Your feed-
back is everything to me, and I don't want to
assume anything anymore when it comes to pro-
tecting our wonderful emotional connection and
communications.
    Now smile, you've got a man who is crazy about
you and that's not going to change.
    With all my love and understanding—Ricky
```

• • •

```
Dear Ricky,
    Come over!
I love you—Bethie
```

The two of them went on from there, building upon the foundation of listening and trust. They continued to enjoy learning how to express themselves with each other. With delight, I noticed a new e-mail tonight from Beth:

```
Hi Jill,
    Wanted you to know that Ricky and I are home
and had a wonderful trip to Italy. His planning
was amazing. We stayed in wonderful villas and
truly saw the country and the spirit of the peo-
ple. Also—you are one of the first people to
know this—Ricky proposed to me and I said yes!
Our togetherness and love is here to stay and
you helped as the catalyst for awareness and
true communication. We thank you, Jill, from the
bottom of our hearts.
    Love—Beth
```

Tears came to my eyes. This couple has proven that we don't have to settle for our old ways, even in the same relationship. Knowing the new way of listening for hidden meanings behind words really works! This is why I love what I do. This is why it is so important to get these messages out to people.

THE OPRAH DREAM

By 4 A.M., I was exhausted. I went back upstairs, got in bed, and closed my eyes. As I started to drift into a semiconscious state, I saw myself standing in a room. There was a woman next to me turned the other way. When she turned around, I couldn't believe my eyes. It was Oprah! I questioned myself. *Was I dreaming? Was I awake?* I couldn't tell. I was, of course, extremely sleep deprived.

Oprah and I started talking and exchanging insights and valuable life lessons. I told the story of my week of insights and about my patients and how they have triumphed over serious illness. She listened with interest. When I told her about how we are doing it all backwards and giving our lives away, she went wild. She wanted to hear more.

Passionately, I explained how we live our lives feeling deprived, not feeling good enough, smart enough, or healthy enough, and how the whole world is waiting for someone on the outside to make them feel good on the inside. I explained to her that we must *take* first, keeping ourselves whole and replenished, and then share from our overflow. She loved this theory, and asked for examples.

"Oprah, the trees take and the sun takes, and all our fruits and vegetables and nuts and berries are an overflow from a life force honoring itself. All of nature works this way and we benefit from its surplus. It's such an easy, automatic process! But people seem to focus on the wrong end—what we *get* from life instead of what we *put into* it." She was excited as I was! She caught onto this theory immediately and added her own insights. We were learning and growing together.

"You are so right," she declared. "I must get a copy of your book." I confessed that the book wasn't complete. She asked me to send her a copy of the book and tapes when they were finished.

As I was speaking with Oprah, I couldn't help but wonder, *Why did I think of her?* I found it somewhat strange. I seldom watch television and I couldn't imagine why *she,* of all the people in the world, popped into my dream. I knew she had a talk show. I read an article once about her struggle with her weight, but why was she connecting to *my* thoughts?

I asked my spirit, *Could Oprah be a catalyst to extend this information to our world?* As we continued to supply each other with valuable information in my dream state, I could see how connected she truly was to spirit. The message read loud and clear. *She is an instrument that can take all information to a higher level.* Then I heard, *Not only will she be helpful in spreading this word, but you, as well, will be extremely helpful to her.*

At that point in my vision, Oprah actually asked if I could help her with her weight problem! She proceeded to tell me her story, which of course, was the story I had read. She shared an experience that had happened when she was fourteen years old. She was about to step onto the bathroom scale when her father walked by. He stopped her and said, "There's no need to step on that scale. You're going to be big." He looked into her eyes and said, "Look at your mamma— she's big—all your aunts are big. They're all big. You come from a big family. Don't worry about that scale, you're going to be big."

She immediately interpreted the word "big" to mean *I'm going to weigh a lot.* She believed those words and has struggled with her weight for her whole life.

In my dream, I said to her, "Oprah, what if the 'big' he meant was that you'd have a really big space for your spirit to grow into? Maybe he was intuitively or divinely guided at that moment? Perhaps he said it without even knowing there was a higher purpose behind those words. This very well could have been the catalyst that was needed to propel you into your search to fulfillment! Perhaps, without that deep and painful void, you wouldn't have reached so deeply inward to learn your life lessons.

"My theory is that by working through these limitations, our spirit stretches and grows. As our realizations grow, we grow bigger spiritually. Maybe on a spiritual level, without realizing it, your father was an instrument that really gave you a gift—the motivation to seek out your *big*, unlimited possibilities. I assure you, as uncomfortable as it may have been to you all through the years, it was truly a gift in disguise. Others can help us create voids, but it is up to us, as individuals, to fill them. Oprah, only *big* people—in the grandest sense of the word—can allow *big* holy spaces to be created within them! It's preparation for our greatness. It sounds as if you came from a spiritually-guided *big* family.

"So please understand, it's not always the way it seems. My interpretation of the true intent behind your father's words is: 'No need to step up on that scale and weigh yourself. You're gonna be a *big person, Oprah,* and I mean *big!* Big in the sense of greatness. Big as in reaching new heights in your own spiritual connection. Big—in every beautiful, positive sense of the word.'

"Oprah, you now have a healthy new meaning, a new interpretation—a new association with that old memory."

This resonated with her. The next thing you know (in my semiconscious sate) Oprah was asking *me* for my autograph. I grabbed a piece of paper and wrote:

Dear Oprah,
My overflow . . . as I continue to live in gratitude for a life well shared,
Dr. Jill

I made a side note—*books and tapes*—to remind myself to send her a copy.

My dream lasted for only a few minutes, although while it was happening, it felt as if we were talking for hours. I got out of bed and started writing. I couldn't get the thought of standing next to Oprah out of my head. By now I knew it wasn't real; I had been in a dream state. But I decided that the dream was a sign, and when my book and tapes were complete, I'd wrap them in a huge, white, shiny box with a big red bow and send them, along with two dozen red roses, to Oprah. I'd attach a card bearing the inscription from my dream.

The next morning felt almost magical as I continued to share my overflow with my patients. They didn't even know about my dream, but each patient seemed to mention Oprah: "You're going to be on Oprah!" This went on continuously! Do dreams really turn into realities? Are the vibrations of thoughts so powerful that through the night they can be carried to so many conscious minds? I do believe that they can be. When spirit talks, I listen. My greatest lessons were the lessons within my very own book—taking and asking for support. I knew to get a book and tapes out to our world, I was going to need a support team. I, as well as many others, am learning to ask for what I want in life. I now realize by asking, I know that I am exercising my spirit on a higher level and walking into my greatness. I was ready to be supported. As I remained the leader of my life, honoring and replenishing myself first, my whole world seemed to follow.

The more I took, the more I became.

The Gift
of Support

When there is cause

in this world, like minds

will align

for the common purpose

of healing

all relationships.

I Was Never Intended to Do This Alone

ALLOWING SUPPORT

My heart was full. The feelings of support were enormous. My Tuesday morning patients flowed in and out. They, too, were excited and feeling connected, eager to hear the next insight. Their responses were very gratifying. As I shared the "experience of the day," they soaked it up, craving more.

The room was buzzing with Oprah ideas when Lisa walked in. Astonishingly, Lisa, who hadn't heard a word about my dream of being with Oprah, said, "Hey Dr. Jill, do you want to go see Oprah with me?" To say the least, we were all shocked. We filled her in.

"Well do you?" she asked. I thanked her for the wonderful offer, but said that with my busy schedule, going to Chicago was out of the question. She countered, "You don't have to go to see her, she's coming here to see you! Oprah's coming to Atlanta for a forum in a few months and I have a ticket for you." I was blown away.

I blurted out, "I could give her my book!" Then I stopped to think. "What book? I haven't written it yet!" We laughed, but the intriguing idea stayed in my mind. At the same time, I knew that even if being with Oprah never happened, just experiencing this outpouring of support from my friends and patients was enough. The commotion finally calmed down and the people left.

I kept thinking about how connected my patients' thoughts were to *my* experience; how the vibrations from my dream must literally have traveled into their minds without words attached! So many of them suggested contacting Oprah before I had even shared my dream. The idea that thoughts can travel to support others stayed with me. Feeling so connected, I relaxed into my creative, receptive mode and wrote:

SUPPORT YOUR THOUGHTS

When there is cause in this world, like minds will align for the common purpose of healing all relationships. Support is essential. You were never intended to do this alone. You have help! You have access to all possibilities. Pay attention to who is supporting your thoughts, for they will influence your outcome. You are a reflection of your peer group and your surroundings. Choose your support wisely. There must be alignment to create growth. You stand simultaneously independent in life and as an individual surrounded by a vast team of supporters. Your path must allow others to assist you to enrich your journey and allow you, in the same way, to be supportive of others.

RISE TO THE OCCASION

My mind deliberated on this theme. I thought: *We are not intended to do this alone. Everyone is a catalyst to help another to a higher level.* I could feel my mind transporting me to a deeper place as I questioned: *Doesn't everyone need support to rise?* At work, at home, and in life, aren't we all supporting each other? Whether we're trying

out for a team or a job, doesn't someone in that field have to recognize our abilities? They then agree to hire us or pick us for the
team, put their signature on our efforts and help us.

We don't have to stop at the point that got us into the game; we
have the option of moving up to a new level. Are we not constantly
upgrading and enrolling a new team of support as we keep acceler-
ating our pace in life? I began to think about our peer groups.
Doesn't our power—or lack of it—sometimes come from the expectations of our peer group? Maybe we all had better start choosing our
circle of friends and co-workers more wisely.

Spiritual Signatures

I envisioned many beautiful souls working together. When they're
ready to grow, they find a catalyst to help them present their efforts
to the world. The established people—the catalysts—give these new
kids on the block a spiritual signature on their soul, helping them to
rise to a higher level.

Isn't that what we're all doing here? Aren't we all catalysts for one
another in the game of life so we can all rise together? Maybe we're
all angels in disguise, lifting each other off our feet as our wings are
warming up to fly.

Don't Run Past the Angels!

It was time to see a patient who had flown in from Philadelphia. I
was blessed to work with Heshie, a magnificent soul who had
founded the "What If" organization. What If puts inspiration and
"possibility thinking" into action for children so they can see the
greatness within themselves. After our session, she asked if Danny
would be interested in writing a song to represent her organization

and its children. I was thrilled, since that's the type of work he loves. I was sure he would be honored to help.

As she continued to explain what she was looking for in a song, the image of a ten-year-old girl named Brittany popped into my mind. Brittany, an extremely talented young lady, had recently written a song for a contest in her elementary school about possibility thinking, and Danny had helped put it to music. I told Heshie about her and asked if she'd like to meet her. "How wonderful it would be to have a song about the potential of children written and sung by a child herself!" she replied.

By some stroke of luck (if you believe in luck), Brittany's mother was home and we went right over. Heshie loved her song and said it would be a great inspiration for What If. Brittany and her mom had hoped and prayed that something wonderful like this would happen. Well, here it was, opportunity knocking at their door!

That evening I received a call from Heshie. Mr. Nobel—yes, *the* Mr. Nobel from the Nobel Peace Prize organization—wanted to meet with her to talk to about a Nobel Peace Prize to represent the possibilities for all the children of the world. With excitement radiating from her voice she asked, "Could we get Brittany's tape so I can take it with me to the meeting?"

We phoned Brittany's mom on a conference call. The whole thing took her by surprise and she immediately began thinking of all the reasons she couldn't follow through on the idea. Her to-do list was endless. "I don't know if we can squeeze it in—the neighbor's child just broke her arm, I need to get to my son's baseball game, and I'm running late. How could I ever get the tape across town tonight, too? It's impossible!" she moaned. She couldn't see the angel's wings of support right there on her own doorstep.

We told her to slow down and take a breath. Heshie explained the impact and possibilities that this could bring to their lives. The bells went off loud and clear this time. She skipped the ball game and delivered the tape. They spent several hours sharing ideas about how to make Brittany's song inspire children across the globe. As you can imagine, this experience made a huge impact on Brittany's life.

The moral of the story was clear: How many times in life do blessings and opportunities come and go because we are too busy? When we forget to slow down and pay attention, these angels pass us by!

ANOTHER MEANS OF SUPPORT:
TRAVELING THOUGHTS

The connections and timing of events continually amaze me. My heart was soaring to see Heshie and Brittany serve as earth angels for each other. I was grateful to be a part of this magical connection. How do people get directed into our lives at the perfect time to help us succeed? Why did they pick that time to show up? Were they guided for a purpose higher than they could have imagined? Are they called together energetically, attracting themselves to each other? Is there a silent channel of communication?

I was beginning to visualize thoughts as magnetic vibrations traveling freely through the universe on a spiritual level. I could see them—thoughts floating back and forth all day just waiting to be picked up by those who will listen. The notion that thoughts travel was engrossing. I began to wonder if some of the information I was receiving was coming from other minds. Were like minds attaching to my thoughts from everywhere simply because I was open and willing to receive?

PICKING UP THE PHONE! SIGNS AND SIGNALS

I reflected back to sessions with patients when the most amazing signs showed up miraculously. I encourage all of my patients to notice the signs around them. I always begin sessions by explaining why I never ignore distractions, such as a ringing phone or a crying child, even during sessions. We need to heal in the real world. If I create a quiet, safe cocoon for patients in my office, when they walk back into their commotion-filled lives, they'll just want to run and hide.

There's a second reason I never ignore distractions. My experiences over many years have assured me that there are no distractions in life. Everything happens for a reason, for our ultimate good. All of these interruptions are signs leading us. My mind traveled back to a time when an older gentleman came to me to help him heal from colon cancer. His daughter and young grandchild brought him over. They asked if they should leave the room. "Absolutely not, please stay," I reassured them. "I'm sure you are meant to be here for an important reason."

I began working with him by trying to help him contact his own immune system. We visualized that his brain was the control center, and that the immune cells in his body looked like little people. His job was to stay in the control center and try to contact his immune team. Unfortunately, he was having a hard time. No matter how I directed him, he just couldn't make the connection. Finally, I blurted out, "Pick up the phone and call them!" At that very same moment his daughter's cell phone went off. He heard the ring and his immune system picked up the phone. That was his first step to recovery.

Thought Vibrations—
Our Other "Telephone" System

His experience with the cell phone got me thinking about the telephone system and how our voice travels. Aren't our phone lines set up to carry vibrations of sound from one place to another? Our telephone system was beginning to look a lot like the thought vibrations I'd been pondering. I couldn't get the parallels out of my mind. The vibration from our voice travels through the phone wire, into the ear of another, then it's interpreted. Maybe vibrations are constantly traveling into our lives and if we are open to them, we can hear them.

Listening to thought or spiritual vibrations was beginning to look like another way of communicating. Perhaps much of our spiritual world is a combination of everyone's collective thoughts. It was more apparent to me that understanding these vibrations would open up the doors for learning. Maybe parts of my week-long experience were becoming clearer. Perhaps in addition to hearing inspired messages all week, I was picking up the receiver and listening to the thoughts of others. Since my mind attracted and welcomed these thoughts and lessons into my "home," they came marching in! As I learned to communicate with the spiritual world, my mind's door—the telephone line—remained open, accessing greater reflections and methods of mirroring. This week it was as if I were in school developing my gifts by learning in an advanced class how to translate the spiritual energy of vibrations. I was getting my master's degree in the language of spirit to help on a higher level in our physical world.

More Confirmation of Heavenly Support

During healing sessions with patients, it has become obvious to me that not only are we guardian earth angels reflecting back to each other, but there are responses back from the universe acknowledging us as well. We're all working together at multiple levels.

I remembered when I was working with Deborah, a patient with ovarian cancer. Her body wasn't able to recognize the cancer, so we turned the tumor into a piece of soft bread. The bread was so soft that she couldn't feel the difference between the soft tissue in her body and the piece of bread. I had her visualize that the sun was heating the bread and turning it into toast. As the bread turned to toast it started to get stiff and she was able to feel it in in her body She continued to toast the bread until it began to crumble.

We then decided to recycle the tumor "bread" for the purpose of good. We called angel birds into her body to eat the breadcrumbs. Just at the moment we called in the birds, a flock of real birds flew over to the window and began chirping loudly. Deborah actually heard them feasting on the breadcrumbs! As soon as the birds inside of her were finished, we thanked them and sent them off. And at the same moment, the real birds flew away!

Another patient, a woman with chronic fatigue syndrome, needed to learn to produce energy within her body. I helped her visualize a storm inside her body that would produce energy. At the very moment we introduced that internal storm, lightning flashed into the room and a real thunderstorm began outside! Our thoughts are so much more powerful than we have even begun to believe!

Many other patients have been in dark places during visualizations and then, when they figuratively came into the light, real sunlight has shined through my window at the perfect time.

DREAM CATCHERS

I remembered an intriguing experience that had happened just two weeks before. My ten-year-old son Andy had invited a friend to sleep over. My seven-year-old daughter Julia looked at me with puppy dog eyes and said, "Since Andy's having a sleepover, can I have a sleepover with you?"

"Of course!" I said. We snuggled up, I kissed her good night, wished her sweet dreams and we fell asleep together. That night I had an incredible spiritual dream about my oldest brother Howard and his wife Gail. In the morning as Julia was waking up, out of nowhere in a cute little sleepy sing-song voice, she said, "Gittle, Gitty, Gitty, Gittle . . ."

This took me by surprise. "What did you just say?" I asked her. "Mommy, what does Gittle mean? Gitty Gitty Gittle . . ."

"Julia, I'm not sure but I think that's your Aunt Gail's Hebrew name." I called Gail. "What's your Hebrew name?" I asked her. "Gittle," she replied, but Howard calls me Gitty when no one else is around." Was it possible that my daughter was picking up the vibrations of my dreams? You never know how your thoughts will impact another or where they are traveling. Be careful what you think about! Inspired by the memory I began writing:

THOUGHTS DO TRAVEL

Thoughts echo through your mind and reverberate into the universe, traveling into the conscious and unconscious minds of others. You are constantly communicating with each other on a soul level, whether you realize it or not. You may receive a thought directly or indirectly and not even know how you acquired it. Be aware and pay attention to what you are thinking, because you are both influencing others and receiving thoughts from others. If you have a compatible energy in your thought pattern it will attach. If not, it will pass you by to attach with another. Thoughts travel aggressively into the minds of others. Like attracts like. If you are thinking positive thoughts, you attract more of the same. If you are thinking dark thoughts, you will attract more dark thoughts to yourself. You have the ability to direct and redirect thoughts. If a negative thought comes in, you have the power to accept it, redirect it or convert it to positive energy and then send it back out again. We are all healers for the whole as we clean up our thoughts.

When your thoughts are not congruent with your desires, the universe will reflect back a situation and a life lesson will be repeated to help you realign your thinking. This way of communication assists your evolution. It's not enough to hope and believe that your dreams will come true—your thoughts and actions must also be in alignment. Only then it will be possible for the universe to reflect back your desired reward. The experiences and people who appear at each moment in your life are there to assist you in getting closer to each of your desires, either by attracting you to what is congruent, or repelling you from what is not. They reflect back to you your current level of understanding and a manifestation of who you are at that moment. Everyone is a brilliant reflection of excellence on a soul level.

I could hear the universe say to me, *What I hear you saying and wanting is this . . .* and then it would immediately hand me the right experience to help me get to where I wanted to go!

NEIGHBORLY SUPPORT SYSTEM

Two patients, Bonnie and Diane, showed up at the same time and startled me. I could feel my spirit jump back into my body.

"Sorry, we didn't mean to frighten you. Are you all right?" they asked.

"I'm fine. I was just deep in thought."

Bonnie had an appointment. Diane, however, hoped I could squeeze her in first to ease her stiff neck.

As I examined her, I said, "Your neck and shoulders feel like you're carrying the weight of the world."

"Yeah, I've had a lot going on in my life." It was apparent that she wanted to chat, and Bonnie immediately offered her an open ear. I finished treating Diane and we spent some time together. Little did Diane know that Bonnie would be stepping in as her earth guardian angel to inspire her and be her role model, mirroring for her who she wanted to become.

MENTORING

The women sitting beside me turned out to be such an interesting and perfect contrast to each other. Sometimes I'm not the only teacher in the room. We're all each other's teachers.

Diane declared that she doesn't have time for this neck pain. Her whole family has depended on her since her husband lost his job years ago and she is the primary provider for the family. "Sounds like you need a break," Bonnie interjected. "Do you ever take a break for yourself?

"Yeah, my two outlets are food and shopping." She looked down ruefully at her midsection. "I've been struggling with my weight for years." She told us she was at the mall today when the neck pain started up. She was shopping for gifts for no one in particular. She loved to give gifts so much that she kept many on hand so she'd be prepared for any occasion.

Bonnie and I looked at each other. Diane was the ultimate gift-giver!

"As a matter of fact, I just happen to have one for each of you. Diane handed us each a beautiful inspirational card. "I love doing this!" she exclaimed joyfully. Diane was the nicest person you could ever meet. We graciously accepted her mementos and thanked her.

Bonnie, experienced in this department, knew what was going on. She reached into her bag and pulled out a lovely sachet. "Diane, I'd like you to have this little gift from me."

"Oh, no," Diane protested. "I couldn't possibly. You shouldn't . . ."

Bonnie looked at me. She knew I knew what was coming.

"But, Diane, you love to give gifts, don't you?"

Diane's eyes lit up with excitement. "I surely do!"

"How does it make you feel when you give a gift?"

"Oh, I adore doing things for other people. It feels so gratifying."

Without hesitation, Bonnie responded, "Then why are you denying others that same pleasure—that same gratifying feeling?"

Diane was surprised. "Why, I never thought of it that way."

Bonnie said, "I understand how you feel. You remind me a lot of how I used to be. I don't have to be a Dr. Jill to tell you how you got that neck pain. Doing so much for others can become a pain in the neck!" She explained how she always loved doing everything for everybody else. Somehow, it seemed she always ended up feeling like a bridesmaid but never a bride.

I said, "But now she *is* a bride! She's a publisher of a local women's newspaper, head of an international women's organization and a public speaker."

Diane said with admiration, "It sounds like you are so directed and self-fulfilled!"

"Yes, I am, but it wasn't always that way."

Just six months before, Bonnie had reached out to me for support. Now, in turn, here she was setting an example to another. I was extremely proud to hear Bonnie tell her story.

Bonnie's first lesson of support was becoming sensitive to the needs of her own body. She had constant back pain when she first came to me. She learned that here was a huge support system even within her own body. She learned how to listen when her back pain flared up. When it was hurting, it was asking her to slow down and redirect her choices. When it wasn't hurting, she was on track. As she healed her back, she learned about teamwork. She and her body were working together, supporting each other. Her next step was allowing people to do things for her, too.

SOLE "SOUL" SUPPORTER: BONNIE'S STORY

"Like you, Diane, I took pride in becoming the sole supporter of my family. Just as you love to connect by giving gifts to people, I get pleasure out of making connections for people and helping them thrive in their careers or in their personal lives. When the love of my life left corporate America to coach people in finding themselves, I wanted to support his dream.

"I thought that by helping my husband as well as everyone else, I was fulfilling my own dreams as well. I didn't realize at that time that I was living only vicariously instead. Everything seemed O.K. until my twenty-eight-year-old son was diagnosed with a genetic connective tissue disorder that was deemed incurable. When his illness was detected, I knew I needed to be strong to support him, too. Suddenly, with this added responsibility, supporting others felt harder than before. So many people were depending upon me for so much support. Of course, I had set it up that way for myself. I began to feel overwhelmed.

U N E X P E C T E D S U P P O R T

"My husband and I had been invited to a private grand opening party at a new restaurant in town. Sonia, a woman at our table, listened supportively to the story of my son's illness. I recall so clearly looking over at Sonia and saying, *I wish I could find a way to help my son.* Although it was hard, I told Sonia that I also needed help. Little did I know at that time that I was sitting right next to one of Dr. Jill's closest friends! 'I know someone who might be able to help you and your son,' Sonia replied. She wrote down Dr. Jill's number on a napkin. That's how I found this angel of support. Since then God has blessed me with so many people who were just waiting to help me. As I learned to pay attention, they instantaneously appeared when I was ready."

S U P P O R T I N G Y O U R S E L F H E L P S O T H E R S

"I looked for support and accepted it," continued Bonnie. "It was one of the most gratifying and difficult things I ever had to learn. In the process of trying to support my husband and help my son find his health connection, the most amazing thing happened—I found myself!"

"I never would have imagined that the journey was not about healing my son, but rather about learning how to ask for and to support my own needs. This difficult experience turned out to be one of those gifts that come in an unexpected package."

Diane asked, "How is your son doing?"

"I'm proud to say that my son is doing so well. He recently got married, and his health has completely stabilized, partly because I started concentrating on my own life instead of on his! It's so amazing. All those years I was trying so hard to help absolutely everybody, never thinking where I was in the picture? Then Dr. Jill taught me how to acknowledge myself."

DOUBLE TAKE: LOOKING AGAIN

Bonnie continued, "I saw myself as the sole supporter of others, and took responsibility for everyone. Diane, I was also weighed down by tremendous feelings of guilt. I'll never forget the day I confessed my fear to Dr. Jill. 'I'm afraid my son may have inherited his disease from me. Even though I don't have this illness, the doctors said it's genetic and can be passed down.' What Dr. Jill said to me came in clear as day and has stuck with me ever since. She told me, 'He has a connective tissue disease, doesn't he? You also love to connect people, right?' I said, "Sure, but what does that have to do with anything?

"Dr. Jill continued, 'Maybe your purpose in life is to help him find the connection. You didn't create the problem. God brought you together because you are part of his "soul"ution. You are a soul supporter of life. You are here to support souls.' "

Bonnie felt the truth of those words. For the first time she learned how important her contribution was to life. Yet at that point, she didn't know how to allow people to recognize this in her; she just wanted to be the helper. "Dr. Jill helped me see that the gifts I saw in others were also living in me. I realized that they can have a dream and I can have a dream, too.

"Dr. Jill pointed out to me that as I became more focused and aware of my ability to take care of myself, I was helping others with my example of personal strength. Now I was having a great time taking care of myself! I didn't even have to try as hard or focus on other people, yet they were benefiting, too. It was amazing! So much easier."

WHAT'S STOPPING YOU?

I said to Diane, "I'll bet you have trouble letting people help you, right?"

"Yes, I guess I do. How did you know that about me? Probably because I'm so much like Bonnie, right?"

"That, plus I know that many people who don't allow others to give them gifts are reluctant to allow people to help them as well. You've already said you think you can do it better and faster without help. That means you don't receive the support you really want because you try so hard to do it all alone!"

"I sure wasn't seeing that before, but I think you may be right."

I told her it was something I was still just learning for myself. "No person was ever intended to do it alone. Give others the pleasure of helping you, just as you will now give them the pleasure of giving you gifts, right?" She smiled and nodded reluctantly. "You're no longer going to say *Oh, you shouldn't have!* That is deprivation thinking, and you deserve the gift!"

"I never thought of it that way."

"Think about this, too," added Bonnie. "Have you ever wondered why people were resistant to your help or advice? We don't realize we're robbing them of the pleasure of self-discovery."

Diane was getting the picture and opening up to it. "What a relief this could be! I wouldn't have to rack my brain trying to figure out what everyone needs. I don't have to do it all by myself. I know I can count on myself, but I can count on you, too. However, neither of us has to be dependent upon the other."

"You've got it!" We gave her a hug. I said, "Welcome! It's an all-about-you day! We are here for you."

All-About-Me-Day

I instructed Diane to sit up tall and follow along with me. "Today is all-about-me day!" I declared. "I am the Queen of my castle and I get to dictate what happens in this kingdom. On all-about-Jill day, people like you are welcome into my kingdom, because helping people like you is what I like to do, and now you become part of all-about-me day. And on all-about-me-day, I like to live in a certain style house and drive a particular type of car, because that's what makes me happy and makes it all-about-me-day. I love being a wife and mother, so spending time with my family is fun because that's also what all-about-me day is about. I decide who is welcome to all-about-me-day and who is not allowed. I only bring things that I like into my world because it's all-about-me day all day every day."

"Sounds a little strong," Diane responded.

"Trust and follow along." I gave her an example. "Let's pretend my children are here and they're throwing a ball. Now that's acceptable because on all-about-Jill day, children are very important. Now by accident, my son throws the ball through the window and breaks it. Well, I say, on all-about-Jill-day, we can't have broken windows, can we! So what do I do? I pick up the phone book and dial 555-fix-a-window because people are available for hire on all-about-Jill day. Within an hour a nice person is here to fix my window. Why? Because it's all-about-me-day all day every day. He does a fine job I hand him a check and say thank you. Then he turns back to me with grateful eyes and says, 'Thank *you*. You just made it an all-about-*me* day, because in all-about-me day, I look for people like *you* with broken windows.' 'You see,' I told both women, 'we are all here to support each other.'"

Diane was ready to get started on healing her own life. During her conversation with Bonnie, they discovered that Diane would be able to help Bonnie with one of her projects at work. It amazed me how, so much like little angels, Bonnie and Diane flew in at the perfect time to help each other rise to a higher level. They were a beautiful part of the greater whole.

Here's a story that reminds me of you two, I said.

I AM SO MUCH MORE WITH YOU

The sun shines so beautifully as it bows down to the sky and says, *Thank you for supporting me. I am so much more with your heavenly space.* And the sun's rays overflow with warmth and light.

The tree says *Thank you* to the sun as it absorbs the light, and it bows down to the earth and says, *I am so much more with your rich nutrients. Thank you for supporting me.* And the tree overflows with oxygen.

A child walks by, takes a deep breath, and says, *Thank you, tree, for your shade and your fruit. I am so much more with your gifts.* And the child grows up and overflows with love for his family and the environment.

The child exhales as the sky bows down to the child and says, *Thank you. I'm so much more because of you. I'm so glad we are one.* And the sky supports the sun once again.

We are all directly or indirectly affected by our willingness to accept responsibility for our journey. We are always sharing and growing, absorbing and recycling for the purpose of helping us all as a whole. Give unconditionally, take for the sole purpose of honoring, and overflow with your gifts. The rest will automatically flow.

We Are All on the Same Team

I told Bonnie and Diane that we're all part of the same energy. We're on the same team. We are one. Your success is my fate. Our lives are interconnected. Be open to see support in ways that you might not have before. It may not come back from the same direction as it went out. Your gifts will come from many different unexpected places.

Recycling Support

I ended my time with them by telling a story a friend named Penny had shared with me. Penny had been diagnosed with cancer and she was taking responsibility for her life. Cancer became her gift because she learned how much power she had in her own healing and her journey inspired her mission to increase awareness about breast cancer. Talking about it took her own fear away. She was determined to help find a cure, and she helped raise money for research.

"The most amazing thing happened," Penny had told me. "Recently, some of my dearest friends walked the three-day cancer walk in my name. I was too weak to walk myself, so I met them at the finish line. At the end of the race, a woman I had never met walked up to me and introduced herself. I extended my hand and said, 'Hi, I'm Penny.' The woman pulled a small piece of paper from her pocket with my name written on it. With tears in her eyes, she gave me a hug and said, "I walked for you!"

The Gift
of Fulfillment

You came here to work your spirit,

not comfort it.

So many want the prize

before they do the lesson.

To achieve the ecstasy

you truly crave,

the growth—step by step—

must come before the fulfillment.

Answers will be revealed

within your voids and

from the reflections of others.

TAKE NINE

My Purpose Here Is to Stretch My Soul

Invigorated, Diane couldn't stop thanking me for all that she had learned in her session about taking help from others and allowing assistance into her life. She exclaimed, "I'm feeling so much better! You know what? I'm so inspired, I'm going to get back on that diet again! I'm going to lose this weight."

"You can do it!" I said. "Come on over if you want support." After she left, I had some quiet moments to reflect. Diane's weight problem got me thinking about the battles we all face with eating too much or shopping too much or taking too much of whatever we use to fill ourselves up—fill in the blank. We're always trying to make ourselves feel better, trying to fill up our voids. But how is that kind of "taking" different from the "taking" that is good for us? I realized that *the former is a way of covering up; the latter is a good way of filling up.*

No matter how many times we make up our minds to change, the test continues. Will we follow the path of least resistance and fall back into our old habits of avoidance and temptation and not even run in the race? Probably, from time to time. However, we will decide to run again, especially if we have a support team in place.

How do we jump the hurdle of our addictions? How do we handle our voids and temptations? I wanted fresh thoughts to pass on to my patients who have tried to overcome their addictions over and over again but haven't succeeded.

By now I had paper lying around everywhere! I grabbed a few sheets and drifted back into deeper places. I was thinking back to those voids from my own childhood—how they felt like open wounds. How I wanted to comfort those open spaces then—the way we all are trying to comfort our holes now. Are they the same holes? I remembered the ecstasy of the revelation that these voids, these sacred spaces—the key to our evolution—were waiting to be filled with pure thoughts. And here we are trying to cover them up! My soul shuddered and it shed a tear when it saw pictures of the toxins we were pouring over and into these blessed openings. As I continued writing, I heard:

FILLING THE VOIDS

You can run, but you cannot hide. Your challenges are your voids—empty sacred spaces your soul yearns to fill with gifts that serve you. Those voids cry out to be filled, to be utilized for your highest good. Many times, when you do not yet have the skills for self-fulfillment, you try to silence that cry with whatever makes you feel better for the moment—food, tobacco, sex, drugs—your anesthetic of choice. You expend energy setting up a barrier between you and your destiny, for you are fearful of showing up in the world as the powerful person you know you are. You try to avoid the responsibility that comes with that knowledge, fearing failure. You will not fail. You were born to succeed. You came into the world to utilize your spirit and exercise your gifts in the physical world. But as long as you avoid this—your main

purpose—you will feel unfulfilled, and you will become
dependent upon your method of escape and comfort.

You came here to work your spirit, not comfort it.
When you crave the temporary solace of addictions,
you're simply doing it backwards—filling yourself up
with rewards prematurely. Your soul is seeking the ultimate high of becoming whole again. So many want the
prize before they do the lesson. To achieve the ecstasy
you truly crave, the growth—step by step—must come
before the fulfillment. Answers will be revealed within
your voids and from the reflections of others.

As long as you do not pay attention to the call of the
voids, you end up falling back into the same old holes,
time after time. Acknowledge the voids; honor them; for
therein await your answers. Your voids are your blessings. Explore the pleasures of filling them with your
soul's requests; then you will feel fulfilled.

Never judge the voids of others or how they are
choosing to fill or cover them. Allow for others as you
allow for your own growth path. No one can fill your
voids for you and you cannot fill another's.

Your soul will always remain under construction and
you will create new cravings. Your stomach will serve as
a constant reminder of your need to fill your voids.
These longings, passions, desires and requests to bring in
the new will enhance your hunger for life. Your digestive
system will assimilate and disperse what you put into
your body and it will inform you when what you have
put in is not in your best interest. Beware of toxins that
taste good and look good but can sabotage you.

HOT FUDGE SUNDAES

Someone opened my office door, making me suddenly conscious of the outside world. It was Tony, coming in for his adjustment. I always enjoy working with him because he loves exploring spirituality and personal growth. I shared some of what I was thinking about—some of my writing. Within an instant, Tony was attached to my thoughts and was flying high.

Then, to my surprise, Diane came in again. "Hi! You're back very soon," I said. She said, "I think I need another 'Jillism.' Can you give me one more, please?"

"That's what I'm here for," I said cheerfully. I introduced the two of them. I told Tony how proud I was of Diane, who was so inspired to start her diet.

"Maybe she'll inspire *me*," he said, patting his tummy. Tony sniffed the air. "What smells so good?"

"Don't ask," Diane said. She sheepishly pulled out a bag holding the leftovers of a triple decker hamburger. She offered us the last few fries from her giant order. "Want some? And we'd better share this before it melts completely . . ." She took the cover off a super deluxe triple scoop banana split hot fudge sundae. "Got some spoons?" she asked. Tony and I tried hard not to laugh, but it was impossible. Diane laughed too. "What's wrong with me? As soon as I committed to this diet, I went out and ate as if it were my last supper. How do you resist temptation?"

"This I gotta hear!" said Tony.

My energy level was rising again. I shared with them willingly:

RESISTING THE TOXINS THAT LOOK GOOD AND TASTE GOOD

"It's easier than you think," I said. "Just avoid the toxins that come in disguises." I turned to Tony. "How many times have you started a diet?"

"Seems like a million," he replied.

"And how much weight have you lost?" I said, turning to Diane.

She started out, "I lost fifty pounds over the last five years . . ."

"That's great!" I said.

". . . unfortunately, it's been the same five pounds—on again, off again," she chuckled. "What do I do about that?"

I said, "Obviously, the problem is not setting the goal or seeing the vision—it's learning how to abstain from the poisons that look and taste good. Think of your stomach as a sacred space, waiting to be filled with good things. You made a choice—a commitment to yourself to eat nourishing foods, right? Let's say you're going to a dinner party tonight. You are motivated, you plan to eat all the right foods, then *wham*, right in front of you is a huge, scrumptious chocolate layer cake. You look at the cake and think, *One little sliver won't hurt me*. As soon as you think that thought, stop and ask yourself this question: "Is eating that cake (or whatever it is) *promoting* my goal or *preventing* it from happening? If the answer is 'preventing,' run—do not eat it. Those are toxins that taste good and will always be around. If you let them seduce you, you'll end up going around and around, getting nowhere fast, like the little hamster on the wheel. Focus on your goal."

RETRAINING YOUR BODY

"Did you know that you have trained your body to ask for what it wants? *Whatever you put in to your body is what you will crave.* Your mind, muscles, organs and all your systems have a memory. You have been programming them—recording onto them—with your behaviors. You've actually trained your body inside and out to ask for what you've been putting into it. Consequently, the good news is you can retrain it to ask for something else! It's time to recondition your body to ask for better things and crave something new— hence better results!

The trick is to take yourself into the voids and to listen to your inner voice—your soul—to find out what it craves most. That craving—your heart's desire—is what will bring you true fulfillment. Just beware of those toxins that look good but can sabotage what you want to become."

"Like hot fudge sundaes," Diane said.

"Right." Then I asked them, "When you're faced with an offering, a decision, or a temptation, what are you going to ask yourself?"

Diane and Tony said in unison, "Will that *promote* my goal or *prevent* my goal from happening?"

"You got it. Ask yourself, *Is this action getting me what I really want?* If the answer is no, simply *do not do it.*"

"That will help," Diane said. "But in the past, I kept trying and trying, but I always gave up on the diet and began eating again. Why? Why can't I stick with it?"

"I just happen to have the answer right here," I replied and pulled out my pages.

"Diane, wait 'til you hear this stuff," said Tony. "It's incredible!"

BE PATIENT WITH YOUR BODY
*Your spirit, innate intelligence, emotions and thoughts
are fast movers. They live in the unlimited. A realization
can take place in a moment. Your physical body, living
in the limited, is much slower. Many times, even when*

the mind and emotions are in alignment with a change you're trying to make, you do not see an immediate response even though it is in motion. Don't get discouraged if the change you're trying to make doesn't happen right away. Stay with the thought and emotions that support the change and allow your body to catch up.

UTILIZING YOUR ENERGY SUPPLY

When your mind creates a thought, your energy level increases to take care of the demand. If you fill these demands in a good way, you grow and achieve because you're utilizing that energy supply. If you create a thought but you're not willing to follow through by putting that thought into action, you create an imbalance. Your energy has increased to keep up with the thought, but you don't know what to do with the excess energy, so you sabotage the thought, and that slows down your energy supply again.

In creating change, do find support, but never become dependent upon it. Support is a catalyst to help your existence become more powerful so you can grow and strengthen on the inside. Beware of letting your catalyst become your "cure." So many times, the catalyst to growth—be it a friend, a therapist, an organization or a substance—becomes the stopping place. It may seem like a cure, but don't be fooled. Catalysts are here to help you learn who you are so you can form a realization that gives you permission to take yourself to the next level. If catalysts are used properly— creating an outcome that allows you to grow without depending upon them—then they are useful. Don't become addicted to your support, for that can prevent your growth instead of promoting it.

Tony said, "Tell us more about how that increased energy supply translates in real life."

"If you create energy, the universe will demand that you use it. Diane, when you dieted and lost weight, you gained energy, right?"

"For a while."

"O.K., so you were revved up and ready to go, but did you change anything else in your life?"

"No, not really."

"So you didn't find a way to use that extra energy. That's why you went back to eating—to fill that new space you created! Tell me," I asked her, "is there something in life that you've always wanted to do, but never did?"

"I always wanted to dance . . . but I always put it off. It seemed I was always too heavy or too tired, or had some excuse . . ."

"There you go! This time, when you lose weight and have extra energy, what can you do instead of eat?"

"I can dance!"

"Absolutely! Fill that empty space with dancing instead of chocolate. When change takes place, it's not enough to take actions without learning a different behavior to take up the space where the old behavior used to live. That's why people fall back into the same patterns and habits—resistance to learning new ways recreates that void. So by all means, ask for what you want, but know that what you're asking for is more than a wish list—it's a responsibility list." She cringed. I smiled. "Responsibility doesn't have to be a dirty word. You can enjoy making your new choices!"

Diane said, "If you say so. But after all my years of trying without much luck, getting started still seems kind of overwhelming . . ."

"It can be, especially because you're programmed to do things for other people. But if that's the case, there's good news. Your energy doesn't know whether you're doing something for yourself or for someone else! Once you get your energy going in the right direction, it grows the need inside of you and keeps on going. Remember, what you put in is what your body craves. So find another reason for feeding your body new energy and just set it in motion."

CREATE A REASON

I have a dear friend, Tammy, who wanted to lose weight. I supported her and gave her advice, but like so many of us, every time she tried, she didn't make it. One day a friend of hers was diagnosed with cancer. Tammy decided to support her by doing the three-day, eighty-mile Atlanta Breast Cancer Walk.

She trained every day, beginning with walking just one mile, until eventually she was up to eight miles per day. One day she came to see me, and she had lost so much weight! The Walk had became the catalyst for her to change. From then on, it was easy for her to stay motivated. However, the only way to truly get to your desired weight and maintain it is to shift your consciousness around your belief system and incorporate the new realization of what "serves" you. Tammy made the change for her friend and now she is reaping the benefits—realizing her possibilities and her worth, doing it for herself!

The trick is to start *somewhere* and get that energy moving in a new direction. Pretty soon your body will be craving the new soul food you are feeding into it. Then your physical body, your actions, and your confidence will be a new reflection to the world of the you that you are feeling inside. Think the thoughts, make the choices, be that person. Actually start treating yourself that way before you even start the program. Do you know what will happen?

You're A Winner Already!

"I'm catching on," Diane said. "When the thought starts, the body will follow!"

"Yes! Here's another hint I want to remind you of, before you leave. You already know it—just apply it. I want you to treat yourself with the confidence that you have already won the race. Years ago, I had an Olympic bicyclist as a patient. He told me that every time he decided to enter a race, he saw himself winning before he ever got out on the course. See yourself as a winner now! You've already got the confidence to do what it takes. All you have to do is go through the motions." Diane and Tony left, eager to implement their goals.

I was glad they were on a roll and ready to get into the race. My thoughts leapt ahead. Once they learned how to resist those toxins, how would they fill their voids, those empty spaces waiting to be filled by good things? What would be their next step in their race toward greatness?

Stretching Past Addictions: Refilling the Voids

I wondered, *How do we honor this process; how do we find our purpose, using these voids to guide us?* The answer was revealed.

> *Allow yourself to be in a constant state of asking for openings, stretching, creating voids, and filling them with your heart's desires. In this way, you are confirming to your spirit, mind and body—and to the universe —that you are in a growth state of expansion. The universe will respond and honor you.*

Of course! We've all been seeking the right thing—fulfillment—but in the wrong way. We've been looking for the treasure but buying the necklace—looking for the quick fix—instead of going on the treasure hunt to find the entire chest.

What this is all about is how to honor our soul's human experience. We're all spirits. This business of getting down to the hard work of learning within our physical limitations—our bodies—is so hard. When we find the fulfillment artificially, we lose our motivation to go back and follow our original path. We accept temporary fulfillment, a feeling that will not sustain itself. We escape into our artificial high, feeling temporary elation until it wears off. Then we're back where we were, or worse, frustrated once again. Our drive is gone and we end up craving only the results driven by the toxins. Even if we're not tempted by toxins that look good, sometimes we want to escape from taking action in the physical world by becoming a spiritual "junkie."

My patient Robin had an incredible dream. She was flying all over the place in heaven, so glad to be back among the heavenly spirits on the other side. They approached her and said, "Why are you so proud to show off your wings? You are so willing to do your work over here, but the real question is—will you do it on earth?" She acknowledged that it was time to spread her wings on the planet.

Maybe we're all wishing to escape the limitations in various ways. We put off jumping over our high earthly hurdles and fill ourselves up with earthly rewards instead, before we deserve them. We keep trying to please ourselves, but unless we're pleasing our soul, it's a masquerade. The work, the struggle—that's what we came for. We're to be congratulated on applying for this job! Nobody said it would be easy. We are all the heroes. We're all here for the human experience—whatever that means to each one of us.

Let's just get to it! Put on our training shoes and get back into the race that we all win. Earn our little awards, step by step, race by race. Action has always preceded results. You've got to get the job before you earn the money, attract the relationship before you earn and create the love. Take away the struggle and you don't get the reward. First comes the motivation to work, then the stretch, then growth will follow, leading into the reward—comfort and fulfillment.

The period of comfort seems all too short, but that's all right, because our soul wants to get on to the next level! It wants to stretch to add to our self-worth. We can gradually build the skills and the momentum we need to win the big races—not racing against each other, but racing for our own goals and finish lines.

The question I had to ask now was this: *If that's the case, how do we make sure we're running toward the right goals? Attracting the right kind of support? Filling our voids with the right soul food?* What had these words meant: *Answers will be revealed . . . from the reflections of others?*

THE NEXT STEP TO GREATNESS: MIRRORING

The whole theory of reflections bounced around in my mind. That's what Bonnie had been doing for Diane—mirroring the qualities Diane aspired to cultivate: focusing on herself and letting go of needing to be doing everything for everybody else. Ricky and Beth were mirroring to each other the communicating skills they wanted to develop in their relationship: staying open and receptive and truly listening to each other instead of closing down. The world's leaders reflect back to billions of people the outstanding qualities they have developed, raising us all to a new level—Princess Diana and Audrey Hepburn, not only for their beauty, but their hearts and compassion as well; Muhammad Ali, who expressed himself so uniquely as The

Champ of the World. Maybe learning from, and being inspired by, others, could be another step toward developing our own greatness?

> YOU CAN NEVER SEE THE GREATNESS
> IN ANOTHER THAT DOESN'T ALREADY LIVE
> WITHIN YOURSELF.
>
> *Look for greatness in all living things and it will reveal*
> *and emerge in you. What is attractive to your eyes you*
> *attract and become. In order to create an expanded reality*
> *and to advance growth, you may seek from the reflection*
> *of another what you desire in yourself. To cultivate the*
> *change, you must be able to acknowledge the greatness in*
> *another before it can be birthed within yourself. If it is rec-*
> *ognizable, it is obtainable. Thoughts can only translate*
> *through the vibration level you have mastered.*
>
> *One way to advance your own process is to mirror the*
> *reflections of others who have mastered that level of*
> *thought. On a physical plane, see the world as a mirror*
> *and emulate like-minded souls. What you radiate from*
> *within will be reflected back to you as confirmation. I*
> *have set your world up in the image of your reflection.*
> *What you see in the world lives within you.*
>
> *The people who appear in your life are your mirror*
> *images. You reflect to each other the progress you make*
> *and your current level of mastery. As you change, your*
> *world changes around you and new people will appear*
> *to reflect those changes. Do not feel sorrow for others.*
> *They are satisfied to progress at their own pace on their*
> *own journey. All journeys are equally valuable. The tim-*
> *ing is unique to each soul. Look to others to remind you*
> *of what you are choosing to strengthen in yourself;*
> *emulate what you deem successful. Whatever you see as*
> *success through the eyes of who you are at the time is*
> *your answer. As you grow, your vision expands.*

I was so intrigued by this concept! However, I knew that we must be careful. The mirroring-reflecting theory works well when we use it positively, but the danger lies in the temptation to remain stuck in the negative form of the thought—envy and jealousy of the success of others—never choosing to believe that those successes are equally possible for you.

THE GRASS IS GREENER

There's a difference between looking at successful role models with curiosity—to see how we might benefit from their example—and wishing we could trade places, which only drives us crazy trying to figure out what's wrong with our own lives. We end up wondering why someone else has it better than we do.

Wishing for something other than what we have can be good if it makes us aware that we have an inside job to take care of; if it is recognition that there is a void to be filled within ourselves. We live our life in order to fill those voids, so if we're feeling restless, it might mean we're ready to make a change.

It's like removing dust from a mirror. By making changes in ourselves, all of a sudden everyone begins to look better. I remember times when I was happy, and it seemed like my husband, children, friends, and patients were also happy. And when I was feeling down, they all seemed down, reflecting back to me, or responding to, my present mood.

DRESS REHEARSAL

Like children playing dress up, we can try on many different outfits in our mental wardrobe until they fit our desires, always being open to change as our mind's styles change.

We can take responsibility to ask *how* to gather information to awaken our own individual greatness. We can seek support from others and achieve the outcome we are looking for by asking *How?* How did they successfully accomplish what we are looking for?

This concept seemed so simple, yet so powerful: To simply copy, reflect and accept.

"Follow the Leader"

Be a copycat! No wonder we're so fascinated by stories of successful people. They, with their accomplishments and fame, in spite of their shortcomings, serve as shining examples for us. When we people-watch, we are observing and admiring with great interest, not only the outcome, but especially the *effort*. When a person wins a contest or makes a goal, we applaud! They accomplish and we get to tag onto their emotion, without the hard work they go through to rise to that level. Or maybe we're previewing what we'd be getting into if we were to go for that same goal. When we watch a performer on stage, we wonder what it would be like to perform before an audience and we feel as if we are a part of their success.

Perhaps we are mirroring when we read books, watch TV, go to movies, listen to the radio and attend concerts. Even if it's not obvious, we are gathering information to trigger emotions we want to experience. It's our way of stretching our emotions and experiencing new worlds that are not always accessible to us or desirable for us. We can use these systems to see how deeply involved we want to be in something new—or if we want to become involved at all.

In a movie or TV romance, when a couple overcomes obstacles to love and reunites, we cheer! Our hearts swell, feeling the emotions we so much want to play with in our own lives. Millions resonated with the movie *Rocky,* rooting for the underdog, experiencing the pain of failure and the hard-worked-for reward of personal success.

Perhaps we can look through the eyes of others, not for envy or judgment, but to generate interest and motivation in our own lives. Maybe the attraction we have to the people who represent "success" to us isn't about "fame" after all. It may be about mirroring for ourselves the next steps in our journey to self-fulfillment. Are we on the right track? What can we do to get to where we want to go? Who do we want to become? By what means can we improve all that we are, so we in return can mirror by example?

I was thinking that the mirroring/reflecting theory works well when you use it positively. The danger lies in the temptation to remain stuck in the negative form of the thought—envy and jealousy of the success of others, never choosing to believe that those successes are equally possible for you.

MIRROR, MIRROR ON THE WALL . . . : BRAD'S STORY

Hmmm, I was thinking, *if the universe sends us mirrors, that means we'd better take an open-eyed look at the people around us who come into our lives.* It could become a detective game to figure out the clues. What are they here to show us about ourselves?

Brad, a patient who's a very talented "starving" artist, came in for his appointment. He had always felt that creativity was more important than money. He became a purist, leaving the family business to be run by his very successful brother, who at the time seemed too materialistic in Brad's eyes.

Brad had enjoyed his group of artistic friends for a long time, accepting their meager pocketbooks. Gradually, he became dissatisfied with the money situation. He helped his buddies willingly, but noticed that they'd always somehow forget their wallet or not have enough change for a cup of coffee. He realized he had set himself up to expect this, but the situation had progressed to the point where he didn't have enough money to meet his own basic needs. He initiated a change: he got a job at a print shop doing graphic design; but he was still dissatisfied.

He sought out my help. I started by showing him what was underneath the cover-up—layers of protection that led to his attitude about money. I began the coaching process by helping him to visualize how he wanted to change.

"Brad," I asked, "who do you admire? Name someone you want to emulate."

"I haven't thought about that, really." He asked me, "Who do *you* admire?"

"I really revere Mother Teresa, for her unconditionally loving heart, her devotional beliefs, and her willingness to see good in everything. I love it when my husband calls me 'Mother Theresa' when I try to help so many people!"

"I guess I don't think that big yet. I could say I really admire my friend Dave—he's such a great artist . . . and Julie—she does beautiful collages . . ."

"Can they pay their bills?"

"Actually, no, not yet."

"I'm not judging them as people. I'm sure they're very talented and nice people. But the question for this moment is—are they the role models you want for your new prosperity?"

"I see what you mean." He was still in the never-never land that comes from not enough thinking.

"Try naming some qualities, then, that you aspire to."

"I really admire self-reliance, being able to be a good provider—kind of a take-charge attitude!"

"Can you think of a person you know with those qualities?" He thought for a moment, then broke into a huge grin. "I can't believe it! I think I just described my own brother. Never in this world did I think it'd ever come to that . . ."

"Brad, this is a breakthrough! Do you realize how important this is? You were trying so hard not to conform that you couldn't recognize those great qualities in your brother. But now that you can, those qualities are ready to be birthed inside of you! This means you've grown. It's not that you want to be exactly like he is, you're just ready find your own path balancing business with your gift of art."

"Cool! I never thought about it like this before." His excitement was building. He was getting into it now.

"Who are some other people you could hang out with and learn from?"

"You know, there is this guy, Ron, who owns his own dot-com company. I really like the way he followed through on his dream. Even if it goes down the tubes like some of the other companies, he gave it a shot. Maybe he'd have an opening for a hot graphics artist! It would be one way to learn the ropes."

"Good for you. Watch him, ask him questions, see how he operates. How does he handle money? Dig inside and bring out those qualities in yourself. Suddenly, you'll discover that you'll automatically begin attracting other people like Ron. They'll show up in the grocery store, at church, they'll notice the change in you and say they didn't realize you were into graphics, or so interested in dot-com companies, or whatever. You'll be surrounded with like-minded people."

"What about my old friends?"

"This doesn't mean you give up your old friends; you just don't buy into their thinking anymore. When your old friends call, you'll naturally and easily detach from the 'not enough' thinking." Brad was seeing the possibilities for himself. "I really want to own and run my own start-up company!"

"Now you're claiming the prize! Go for it! See it and project it. I strongly suggest that you never say 'I can't do that' anymore. Never say 'That will never work.' Always try and try again! Step by step, change and change again if something's not working. Direct and redirect! It's like finding yourself in the middle of a cornfield. The cornstalks are higher than you are and you can't see behind you or in front of you. All you can do is push them out of the way, stalk by stalk, step by step. You know the prize is there for you. Say 'I'm going to get it!' then push the obstacles out of the way. If you're not finding what you're looking for, turn in another direction and push your way through on another path. You'll find it."

"You make it seem so possible."

"It *is* possible! In fact, I should introduce you to Sherrie. She started out as an accountant but is now following her dream of being an artist, against her parents' wishes."

His eyes lit up. "Good for her."

"I thought you'd like that part. In fact, their reflections back to her were so strong a block that we did a visualization to release them. We turned her mom's and dad's expectations into antique furniture and placed them into her abdomen, her 'house.' She had to decide if the furniture, as valuable as it was, suited her needs. Her answer was clearly 'No.' She was a contemporary girl. So, we called the spiritual good will center to send down a truck and we gave away all of this valuable furniture. She filled her "house" instead with a beautiful studio. Brad, you'll never guess what happened! When we finished her visualization, there was an Allied Van Lines truck right outside my window! I kid you not. The universe has a sense of humor! It was mirroring confirmation that she was making the right "move!"

"I'd like to end the session by sharing this with you," I said. We read together before he left.

> *You can never see what you don't own. All reflections, positive and negative, are images of self to help you recognize what lives within you and what you are projecting to the world. They are instruments for realigning and adapting choices. One might see through the eyes of the child or set the mind into a dream state to plant the seeds of curiosity. Could my life be better or different? This creates space for growth. The picture of what could be is set up in the likeness of the magnificence that dwells in others and also in you.*

> *What I love about you is what lives in me.*

> *What I see in you is what I can see in me.*

> *What I know about you is what I know about me.*

UNWRAP THE GIFT OF YOUR SOUL

Seeing the world anew as a huge mirror of our own greatness raised another question. How did our sense of greatness ever get lost? I know we are all born with the highest and best within our soul. If the highest and best is always present, then why can't we recognize it? Aren't we here to honor the qualities that are worthy to our soul?

I began to reflect back to when my children were babies. Barebottomed, their truth was exposed. The most amazing pure, whole and complete packages had been delivered. Their authenticity—their soul—was revealed. We were so proud, and they were so lovable and they knew it!

Maybe we came into this world like the sun, knowing how to honor ourselves and fulfill our soul. We took to replenish our growth; our warmth, joy, and happiness automatically spilled over to all, like the rays of the sun—until one day someone told us we were doing it wrong; we were selfish.

It didn't make sense to think of ourselves as less than we had been, so to protect our soul, we wrapped it up with layers of protection to guard its beauty. We were trying to save it from harm. We padded our joyful soul with layers of doubt, guilt, fear, avoidance, withholding, the need for approval and the need to please. What we have been seeing in others and shrinking away from—the defenses, the walls—are also our own layers. We believed we were protecting this magnificent essence we brought into this world; then one day we figured out that all we're doing is preventing it from shining and sharing.

My adrenaline started flowing. I was thinking about how ready our world is to promote the godlike qualities inherent within all of us once again. How ready we are to expose our greatness and unwrap the protective layers to show the inherent beauty of our souls once again.

The moment has come. We must teach, live, and treat each other on a soul level. I was certain that as I saw and mirrored the highest and best in my patients, they would see it in themselves again, see it in others, and reflect that shining example for others to see. In turn, we would all begin treating each other with the highest regard. I could see this message taking off like wild fire and spreading to all!

Our Image Reflects a Long Way

My mind traveled back to an evening when I was at a party with my husband. A woman I had never met before approached me. "I want to thank you," she said. "You changed my life forever. You don't know me; I'm a friend of one your patients. She shared your lessons on how to honor ourselves." With tears in her eyes, she said, "For the first time, I believe in me."

What a beautiful confirmation from the universe! I felt like a mom watching her child succeed. I knew with a full heart and a proud smile that my commitment and willingness to share my message was off and running. Just by honoring self with clear intent and overflowing from abundance, even without being present, one person's truth can spread throughout our world!

Little did I know that my bubble was about to burst . . .

The Gift
of
Remembering

In the infinite world of possibilities,

you are one of them.

It is extremely hard to enter into

this experience—

a one in a million chance

of even entering this world.

You are winners already

just by making it here!

We Had It Right All Along!

The shock of venturing out of my inner sanctuary into the real world was almost more than my body and spirit could handle. For five nights and six days I had floated intensely in the sacred angelic space of timelessness, feeling incredibly connected to my soul and to the divine. It was time for reentry. I needed a breath of fresh air and sunlight. I took a quick lunch break and headed to the local sandwich shop.

THE CHILDREN

What a jolt! The noise, the roar of traffic, honking horns, radios blaring—all drowning out the gentle voices of our souls. I stood in line for my veggie sandwich. A woman in front of me yanked on her children, scolding them loudly. I'm one who loves people, but in this moment, like the others in the shop, I wanted to shield myself from this assault on my senses. Then my protective instincts for the children were aroused.

She said loudly, "I am not buying you the lunch with the toy. You have too much already!" I watched the kids cower from her words. Her tone grew louder, "Buy me, get me, give me, take me, that's all I hear from you all day long!" She blared, "You're so spoiled!" The children broke down into tears. "Don't you realize there are poor children who don't have any toys? You don't even appreciate what you have. And you'd better not let any of your food go to waste. There are starving children in the world!"

We were all cringing. I grabbed my sandwich and ran outside to sit under a tree. My intent had been to relax and enjoy a nice, quiet lunch, but I was shaken. The disrespectful treatment of those children stirred so much up inside of me. This was not the way to teach values to our young.

MAKING YOURSELF LESS
DOES NOT MAKE SOMEONE ELSE MORE

I couldn't get those words out of my mind: *Don't you realize there are poor starving children in the world?* My adrenaline was flowing. I was on a mission. What are we doing to our children? It hit me like a lightning bolt. *We are leading our children into deprivation thinking.* This thought triggered something deep within me. *You can never make anyone more by making yourself less.* Of course we want to teach our children about the less fortunate, but how in the world can making our children feel worthless feed the starving children in Nigeria?

Obviously, the message this woman was trying to get through to her children was, *Appreciate what you have; understand and be aware of what's going on in the world.* What she didn't realize was that her children heard: *I'd better sacrifice myself in order to help someone else.* The mother was trying to instill values by telling them, *It's not always a good thing to have everything we want handed to us.* But the children interpreted her anger to mean, *I'd better not ask for what I want or I'll be spoiled and bad.* The children ended up feeling guilty for wanting something. I felt such sadness and outrage. I wanted to scream out, "IT IS NOT O.K.!" Talk about doing things backwards . . .

MIXED MESSAGES

Even those who do not treat their children that way have occasionally fallen into the same type of thinking: "Better eat everything on your plate; there are less fortunate children who don't have what you do." We want the best for our children and have the best intentions; however, that isn't the message we always convey. We believe we're doing the right thing, but unconsciously we're devaluing our children with our words. We're actually setting them up for low self-worth, making them feel guilty for even asking, or making them feel guilty for their choices.

HANDING DOWN THE WOUNDS

We inadvertently minimize the thinking of the young, leading them into deprivation mentality. Initially, I felt sympathy for the children and anger at the mother. Then I realized that someone must have treated the mother that way and taught her that way of behaving, and I immediately felt compassion. She was that little child at one time. I questioned where the whole cycle of not feeling worthy begins.

A picture flashed through my mind. I saw my adult patients, like that mother, as wounded little children flooding into my office. I could see them inheriting "wounds" from their ancestors, then bringing them in to me to help them heal them. One by one, they handed over their way of thinking and behavior; straight down the line it went, from parent to child, generation to generation, wound after wound. I felt such emotion, thinking how it starts in a line in a sandwich shop. I wished that I could find a way to help everyone do it differently and stop the cycle of low self-esteem.

We must treat our children with respect. Wouldn't it be much better to remind our children that they are the future to all possibilities? That their worth and capability come from learning to accept responsibility and make good choices for themselves? That as they raise their own standards, they will have the ability to help others raise theirs as well? If children feel guilty and deprived, they'll be so needy that they won't feel like helping anybody else. Instead of blaming them for not thinking of starving children, couldn't we show them instead how to take action and send donations?

GIVING AND RECEIVING TOO MUCH?

I reflected back to my own life, my children, and my childhood. I, and my parents, are guilty of the opposite—giving our kids too much. Why is it so hard to resist buying them everything? How does this happen? I wondered. I could literally hear my mother's voice echoing in my mind: *I want you to have everything I didn't have as a child.*

In a flash, I realized, *We're trying to fill our childhood voids through our children.* No wonder it boomerangs. Our kids don't have the same voids we did. My mother didn't receive very much and wanted us to have much more than she did, so she inundated us with gifts and toys. Parents see this as giving and children see it as endless receiving.

I asked myself, *Is this the right way to determine how much to give? Maybe we're teaching them to expect too much and to act up when they don't get what they want.*

RED LIGHT, GREEN LIGHT 1-2-3

We can dish it out but we can't take it! We're great about giving to our kids relentlessly, but when they ask for something . . . "Hold it right there!" we shout. We draw the line and say, *That's enough!* We train our children to receive all the time by our giving, giving, giving. Then we turn around and get angry at them for asking. We're giving them mixed messages, teaching them it's not O.K. to ask. *Red Light/Green Light. Stop and Go.* Have we been training them this way without knowing it? My mind continued to question this endless receiving and giving. I wanted to find out if there is a difference between *receiving* and *taking*.

"YOU MAY TAKE THREE GIANT STEPS ...MOTHER, MAY I?"

Endless giving on the part of the parent is acknowledging work that is never done. Handing out rewards and answers prematurely slows down the stretch, the drive to learn. Doing so robs our children of the satisfaction of self-discovery and built-in awards for achievement. Thinking about the reward without understanding the steps necessary to get it results in failure! *Taking* implies responsibility. *Taking* is an Action Step.

Some children want grades without effort. Maybe when we help with the homework, they get good grades and believe they deserve them, but when we aren't there to do it for them they fail and feel disappointed in themselves. The result: low self-esteem—*I'm not good enough!*

How will children grow to become inner-directed if we keep doing everything for them? If we keep giving them mixed messages? If they lose their inner curiosity and motivation, they will lose their ability to solve their own mysteries and may become lost on their journey. The major benefit of the gift of taking is becoming responsible for our own choices and learning from those decisions. Maybe our gift to the children can be to teach them how valuable and capable they are. We can express confidence in them and show them how to succeed by taking action steps toward their goals.

I smiled to myself. The big PG sign came into my head! The movie rating Parental Guidance isn't PC—Parental Control. None of us—adults or children—wants to be controlled.

I was ready to do my part. It was time to get back to work.

A Child Who Loves: Christopher's Story

Christopher arrived at my office in his mother's arms. I so enjoyed working with this nine-year-old boy, who radiated pure love, pure passion, and pure excitement about life. I had met him while I was on vacation a year before.

At that time, my practice was flooded. Helping people who are challenged with illness has its rewards, but I knew it was time to recharge and take a break. My husband suggested that we take a weekend off at the lake with our friends. Just what the doctor ordered, I thought—a quick getaway with Danny and the kids. We were lounging by the beautiful lake hotel pool, chatting with our friends. Out of the corner of my eye, I saw Christopher wobbling toward us. Our friends greeted him with open arms. Christopher's mom and dad joined in the conversation.

Danny asked Christopher's parents about him. Cheryl, his mother, explained that he had a severe case of muscular dystrophy, a degenerative muscle disease, and had difficulty walking. Danny turned to me immediately and said, "Hey, Jill, what do you know about muscular dystrophy?" I smiled up toward the heavens and said, "O.K., God, guess that break was long enough. Here we go again." I took a deep breath and the next thing you know Cheryl and I were entrenched in conversation about health and healing. I could see her eyes fill with emotion as we talked. "Your theories on healing make so much sense. You're the first person who has given us a reason to hope," she said. "How soon can he start?" Now here we were, one year later, and Chris had made much progress.

Christopher was ready to heal his life and take responsibility right from day one. He had the right idea out of the starting gate. I'll never forget what happened after his very first treatment. He trusted his inner voice—his own instincts—which helped him win the race.

THE BRAIN FACTORY

When Christopher first began seeing me, I knew he was a truly old soul who was here to learn on a higher level. He caught on so quickly. Christopher's problem was that his body didn't produce a protein called *dystrophin* that enables muscle contraction. His muscles atrophied over time. We decided to do a kid-friendly visualization to create a plant manager who lived in his brain. He would run the factory that produced dystrophin. We named him Mr. Dystrophin. His job was to supply Christopher's body with dystrophin and send it into the muscles to make them strong again. We set up his muscles to look like little kids.

Christopher's job was to talk to the kids and ask them daily if Mr. Dystrophin was doing his job. If all systems were go, they'd hold up a GO sign. If not, they'd hold up a STOP sign. Then it would be Christopher's job to go and talk to Mr. Dystrophin again and remind him of his duties. I told him his heart would have to be strong to talk firmly to this big plant manager. He caught on immediately and he was having so much fun playing inside of his body. I reminded Christopher before he left, always watch for the signs and take heart.

THE RACE

On Christopher's next visit, Cheryl raced through the door with him. She said, "The most amazing thing happened last night! I'm sure it was a sign." She was almost too excited to speak. I was on the edge of my seat wanting to know what had happened.

"Christopher woke up calling out for me in the middle of the night. He had the most surprising dream! He dreamed that his heart and his mind were in a race. I asked him who won."

He said, "My heart, Mom. My heart won!"

"It's amazing," she said. "He never talked like this before." For the first time I could see true hope in her eyes. Christopher received the message right from the start. It didn't matter to him from then on how many doctors or others would say something discouraging to him from their "heads," he knew the heart would know the truth and his heart would always win.

PERMISSION SLIPS

Christopher's visit today turned out very special. He was to be the catalyst for a very important insight. He worked diligently on his healing and we finished up a few minutes early. He, his mother and I were all talking, when suddenly Christopher said, "Mom, before I forget, you need to sign my permission slip! My class is going to the zoo next week."

"Of course . . ." I exclaimed, ". . . the permission slip! Chris, you may not realize it, but you just gave me one of the greatest insights of all." Cheryl and Christopher were all ears. "I think I just figured it out—how we all got into this 'not-enough' state of mind. Why we need approval so much and why we became so dependent on everyone else to give us our answers. *The permission slip!*

"Cheryl, remember when we were kids like Chris and our whole class was going on a field trip? We'd storm into the house and flash that permission slip right in front of Mom or Dad and say, pretty please can I go? Mom and Dad said of course we want you to have everything and enjoy all the good experiences, so they signed off and we'd get to go and have fun. We learned at a very early age that we must get permission from authority to get what we want. As children we needed those boundaries and guidance, but as we grew up, we forgot to put that permission slip back inside of us where it belongs. We're still waiting for someone to sign off and give us permission to get what we want in life! The only permission or approval we need to make positive changes in our lives is *our own!*"

"You're right," Cheryl said thoughtfully. "I'm ready to sign my own permission slips." Christopher left feeling so proud once again, for he had contributed to another amazing insight.

We keep listening for all the signs and signals, and we continue to hold the intention for a full, healthy life for Chris.

BLESSINGS FROM ABOVE

My mind and thoughts were still full of the innocence of children when my last patients of the day arrived, Laura Beth and Andrew, a young married couple coming in for their monthly adjustments. I was delighted to learn that they had just found out their first child was on the way! A new little blessing, so fresh and pure. My heart swelled with love for their new child; for my own children; for all the children of the world. I was sure they would be inspired by one of the messages I had received and had written down in the wee hours:

> ### YOU ARE WINNERS ALREADY!
> *Deep within the universe is an endless number of lessons and options. We have access to all opportunities before choosing this life. The universe, like a toy store, holds many games filled with various laws, levels and principles. Life as we know it here is only one learning experience from which to select. In the infinite world of possibilities, you are one of them. Learning from life lessons will now and forever be one of the most challenging and rewarding growth periods of all. It is extremely hard to enter into this experience—a one in a million chance of even entering this world. So you are winners already just by making it here!*

Laura Beth and Andrew were moved—thinking about the power of their baby-to-be. An idea came to me.

Laura Beth and Andrew were both very clear about the effectiveness of visualization. They always delighted in remembering how Laura Beth brought Andrew into her life that way. A couple of years before, she had been single. She and I worked together on manifesting a relationship. As she learned to release her old illusions around men, she became extremely clear about what she wanted in a relationship. She worked religiously, creating very specific images in her mind of her perfect mate. A year later, he walked into her life. He was exactly what she had envisioned— sensitive yet powerful, handsome yet filled with direction and spirituality.

I asked them today, "How would you like to do a welcome-into-the-world visualization to honor you, the new parents, and your baby-to-be?" They were thrilled with the idea.

ANGEL BABY

Laura Beth and Andrew sat in comfortable chairs, relaxed, and closed their eyes. I told them take a deep breath and unwind. Listen to my words as you focus on your breath as it flows in and out of your body. In with the good, *take a breath in,* keep all that you need, *feel your body holding on to it for as long as it serves you,* then overflow lovingly, exhale, knowing the new will continuously and constantly flow into your life, *cleansing breath in and out.*

I then helped them create an image in their minds. *Envision a beautiful Heavenly Angel Baby filled with all of life's greatness floating freely through the universe looking for two beautiful souls who are open and willing for love to come in.* They saw the angel baby clearly. *Feel your spirits cradle each other creating an enchanted space for your new baby's soul to enter.* Andrew reached over to hold Laura Beth's hand. *Beautiful Angel baby, child of Laura Beth and Andrew, as we bless you, we thank you for serving as a constant reminder of who we are as well.*

I envisioned all the lasting impressions that I received throughout the week and shared them with the spirit of the child. Suddenly my level of awareness began to increase. I could actually see the angel baby approach us. I spoke to it:

> *Angel baby, as you enter into this life all your features and gifts will go inward.*
>
> *The circle of light from your halo will become the **crown** on the top of your head to serve as your constant reminder that you are royalty, valuable, significant, and worth it all!*

*Upon the soles of your feet, your "soul"—**footprints**—will
be placed to remind you that you are always choosing the direction of your own path.*

I could see the beautiful angel baby enter the womb, tucked safely
away, getting ready for its new adventure. I took a deep breath.

*Heavenly Angel Baby, your angel wings will go inward and
they will become your **lungs**, and with every breath that you
take, will be reminded that you are now flying as an earth angel!*

Laura Beth and Andrew were flying high. Andrew gently leaned over
and kissed Laura Beth on her forehead. Laura Beth leaned over and
said, "I love you both so much!" They vowed to bless the baby
through each stage of development and to always remind themselves of their greatness at the same time. They floated out the door.

My workday was complete. I couldn't help but think of my husband and my two beautiful children who also served as reminders of
who I am. So inspired, still in an angelic mood, I was feeling so
honored and blessed by the thought of our children choosing us to
be their parents. I couldn't wait to go home!

H O M E   A G A I N

My children and I embraced as I ran into the house. They climbed
onto my lap. I asked, "Before you were born, did you pick me to be
your mother?" Julia paused only for a moment then said innocently,
"Before I was born, I asked for a mom who was kind and nice and
pretty." Andy chimed in, "I asked for a mom who was sweet, fun, and
really cool . . ." They giggled and jumped off my lap to go play. Julia
stopped suddenly, turned back to me and said, ". . . and I got just
what I asked for." Andy winked.

Full Circle

My spirit felt like it had come full circle. Through the eyes of a child, I could see the truth clearly. We came into this world with total abundance and knowingness. Then we went into deprivation. We spent our whole lives trying to get back to where we started! It was time to start from the beginning and work our way from the inside out expanding, growing, and learning. The world is in the palm of our hand as we trust ourselves first and foremost, allowing our lessons to come freely as we value our mind, soul and body. As we focus on our goals and stay flexible along the way, we feel privileged to take all that life has to offer. As we welcome all the changes and constant resistance, we know we are being challenged to stretch to the next stage of learning as we evolve. I was eager to shout these words to the world. *We are doing it backwards! It can be so much easier!*

I knew this message was an idea whose time had come.

The Birth of a New Idea

Height—The Eternal Heavens

Length—The Infinite Universe

Time—Ageless

Weight—Lifting the World off Our Shoulders

It appeared so pure and simple, yet felt so powerfully driven. Like a once-upon-a-time story, there I was, gazing into the looking glass. The gift so magically appeared: *The power always lived within me, within all of us.* Honoring self is enough to attach all possibilities to our outcome. It's my turn! It's everybody's turn! Our responsibility is to honor and respect ourselves above and beyond anything else, to replenish ourselves always with the gift of taking. We are priceless. We came into this world pure, whole and complete with all our gifts just waiting to be revealed. We are the gift to be cherished!

THE SIXTH NIGHT

On the sixth night, my friend Randi stopped by in early evening. She suggested that I explore the idea of starting a web site and urged me to see if the name of my "domain" was available. I told her I didn't have time just then. She offered to set it up on my computer and left me simple instructions for when I was ready.

Later that evening I reflected back to this experience feeling joyful and elated. I remembered how I had watched the sun rise and had given thanks and said with amazement, "Had You stopped right here it would have been enough! But then You went ahead and blessed me with so many new days filled with wonder and revelations." In my eyes, every day was a bonus. When the house was quiet, I said, "I am so grateful for all You have shared and given to me. I am full."

Everyone else was asleep. I turned on the computer and opened up the page Randi set up for me. I'm not too experienced using the Internet, so I was grateful for her simple instructions. "Type in the name you want, but do not leave any spaces in between." Sounded easy enough.

I had been given ten chapters from the universe and ten lessons to follow for honoring ourselves and enjoying life. So I decided to see if the name "The Universal Laws" was available. I thought I was typing "THEUNIVERSALLAWS" and by "mistake," (or driven by spirit) I typed an "O" in Laws instead of an "A." As I read it, I couldn't believe my eyes. It said, "THEUNIVERSALLOWS." The universe allows. At that moment, I realized that the true gift was revealed. It was *not a law* of the universe that we needed to follow; it was *an allowance if we chose to take it.*

I sat down and wrote out the ten universal allowances.

THE SEVENTH MORNING

I felt so fulfilled. I walked downstairs and Danny was standing in the kitchen. He asked with concern, "Could you sleep at all?" I looked up at the heavens and then back at Danny. I smiled and responded, "God said thou shalt rest on the seventh day . . . and I did!" The book was complete. I rested. He picked me up in a wonderful hug and we twirled around, laughing! The children joined in the merriment. Their mommy was "home" again.

The Ten Universal Allowances

Allow Yourself To ...

Take responsibility and honor yourself first

Stay inner-directed and trust your inner voice

Balance with the body's wisdom to create total wellness

Be receptive and stay in choice

Recognize self-value and overflow true worth

Allow freedom for others as you allow it for yourself

Listen for the intention behind the words

Accept the hand of another for support

Crave learning and seek fulfillment

Remember through the eyes of the pure inner child and use the world as a mirror

Aftertakes

The Big
Picture

THE BIG PICTURE

Long ago, but not far away, a single strain of life force
filled with purpose joins with another to lend it support.
With meaning, it gains added dimension by expanding its realities.
Strengthening by means of wisdom, privileged with the properties of
attraction, it maximizes its inherent power and charm.
It allows all that will provide for, nourish and replenish it to approach.
It lives with pure intention to strengthen and promote its growth.
Guided by internalized values, it relies on and trusts its innate intelligence within.
Believing in and relying upon its integrity, power and ability, it remains confident.
Staying true to the obligation and responsibility imposed from within, giving itself permis-
sion to continue, without fear it moves forward.
Faithful to its allegiance, it stays enthusiastic to its commitment.
It functions by holding its structure as a means of sustaining life.
Understanding its value, it serves as a stage of foundation.
Allowing support and being supportive, embraced with many and all skills, it branches into
learning, to gather and distribute information, using its capacity for reasoning.
Living in abundance, it views all information as a benefit.
To maintain its balance it replenishes continually,
overflowing its surplus as shared gifts—
gifts to be recycled to attract to all who will benefit.

• • •

With God as my partner, the womb of my mother contracts,
my reminder that I made a contractual agreement to remember my responsibilities.
I proceed down the birth canal to present my crown of honor!
Immediately acknowledging my worth as I approach the world,
the doctor takes notice and shouts for all to hear,
"The baby is crowning!"
The royal value is understood from the very first appearance of life.
Feeling loved and appreciated, purposeful with meaning,
strong and wise, attractive and charming, nourished and healthy,
supported and supportive, intentional and powerful,
filled with integrity, inner-directed, responsible,
confident and secure, faithful and committed,
functioning and productive, valuable and compassionate,
safe and trusting, intelligent and abundant . . .
Pure Love: The Child is Born
We come into this world, a small contained replenishing body
of importance that honors and directs its own universe,
as we act a part within a larger universe.
The Gift of Life

Lasting
Impressions

LASTING IMPRESSIONS

All the answers are within you . . .

You came into this world ready to take the earthly challenge. Reminders were carefully placed within your mind, body and soul, to help you remember your responsibilities to yourself and who you truly are.

This chart of lasting impressions, inspired by my week-long experience, will remind you of the greatness that lives within you. When you forget how to honor the true intent of your soul—reaching for your highest and best self—symptoms or illnesses "show up" to help you redirect your choices, allowing you to get back on track.

Use this chart to learn what each of your lasting impressions represents and what it is trying to tell you. Your life will become so much easier as you learn how to listen and reconnect to your whole self.

Please feel free to use this information in any way that inspires you. The lasting impressions may be used as affirmations—reminders, clues, confirmation and insights.

Here are some suggestions:

Refer to this chart to reinforce your greatness, to remember all the gifts you brought with you into this world. Discover the power within you. Allow different areas in your body to help you focus on what you want to strengthen in your life. Then recall a time when you felt powerful and pull that memory-feeling into that part of you.

If you feel pain, out of sorts, or ill, use the constant reminders to positively remind you of what you need to balance yourself. You can reinforce that by saying the reminder several times a day.

Focus on your solutions, not on your problems or symptoms. (Example: If you are having lower back pain, by focusing on the problem it may increase the pain. Instead, focus on the affirmation to help you rebalance and heal.)

Honor yourself by accepting compliments graciously when people notice your inherent qualities.

Most of all, thank your body for working together with you and communicating its needs. Take care of yourself, encourage yourself, and create enjoyment while learning and expressing yourself.

Enjoy your life!

LASTING IMPRESSION	REPRESENTS	YOUR CONSTANT REMINDER
Arms	Willingness to take for yourself and give to others	*You are capable of reaching out to obtain all that life has to offer.*
Belly button/ Umbilical cord	Your first means of support	*You were never intended to do it alone; you trust that you will always be provided for and life supports you.*
Body	Your home, your kingdom, your sacred space for learning	*You are a powerful individual who holds the privilege of controlling your own mini-universe.*
Brain/ nervous system	The house for your thoughts	*Utilize your wisdom, communication skills, and understanding to be responsible and creative with your thoughts, choices and beliefs.*
Connective tissue	The common thread that connects your life	*We are all interrelated; we are all linked to all living beings.*
Crown of head	Your opening to worth	*You are a royal being; you are valuable, significant, worthy and important.*

LASTING IMPRESSION	REPRESENTS	YOUR CONSTANT REMINDER
Ears	Your interpreters	*Hear openly and with flexibility; listen to understand the intentions behind the words.*
Emotions	Your steering wheel	*Pay attention to all your feelings. Use them as your feedback system, signaling you if you are on or off course, so you can redirect your choices.*
Endocrine system	Your inner emotional centers	*Allow all your feelings to be expressed as you become aware of what they are telling you.*
Eyes	The mirrors of your soul	*See with insight, sensitivity, and clarity as they mirror lessons to you and, in turn, reflect your soul back to the world.*
Fat	Layers of protection	*You are safe, cushioned, and shielded from harm.*
Feet	Freedom of choice	*Your "soul" was placed on the bottom of your feet so you always have choice of the direction of your own path.*
Fingerprints	Your individuality; your uniqueness	*There is nobody else exactly like you, and you have come to put your individual stamp upon the earth. You will remember that there is no one right way; allow for the differences in yourself and in others.*

LASTING IMPRESSION	REPRESENTS	YOUR CONSTANT REMINDER
Fingers	Your tools	*You have a variety of instruments, methods to accomplish your desires.*
Hands	Your ability to take action to grasp what you want in life	*You are worthy of taking hold of what you desire and giving what you deem valuable.*
Head	The vault that stores your valuables	*All your thoughts are safe within. This is your divine chamber to express privately.*
Heart and circulatory system	Exchange system for change	*All of life is a constant cycling and recycling of energy. As you remain in balance, health, inner peace, and success will become a natural progression of events.*
Immune system	Your internal bodyguards	*You have many strong and healthy aspects of self that resist sickness and attract health.*
Innate intelligence	Your internal God energy	*You are in partnership with God; your internal world runs automatically accepting all the choices that you contribute as truth.*
Intuition	Your true original inner voice	*Come from the power of trusting your inner self and inner partner above all else.*

LASTING IMPRESSION	REPRESENTS	YOUR CONSTANT REMINDER
Liver, gall bladder, bowels and rectum	Your centers of cleanliness	*You always have a safe place to remove toxins from your life, leaving you pure, whole and complete once again.*
Lower back	The pivotal point in your body for support and balance	*Remain balanced, calm, and stable.*
Lungs	Deservability centers	*You are worthy of taking all of life in and expanding. Your angel wings go inward and with every breath, you fly as an earth angel.*
Muscular system	Point of strength	*You are powerful, influential and an authority in life.*
Nose	Fulfillment and your path to abundance	*As freely and easily as you breathe, there is more than enough, prosperity, health, inner peace, happiness, and all of life's bounty—in unlimited supply, just waiting for you to take it in.*
Pancreas	Your sweetness	*You are worthy of having a sweet life, sharing and receiving kindness, compassion, sympathy, consideration and concern.*
Reproductive system	Your importance	*Use honorable intentions and only those thoughts, ideas and actions that you deem valuable and are proud to replicate.*

LASTING IMPRESSION	REPRESENTS	YOUR CONSTANT REMINDER
Shoulders	Your power point of endurance	*Always stand tall as you endure life's challenges.*
Skeletal system and joints	Your structure, stability and agility.	*Your life is in perfect order. You are connected, united with form—stable and organized, yet alert, lively and flexible.*
Skin	Holds your internal world together	*You are embraced and surrounded by a life that is held together tightly.*
Spirit/Soul	Your purpose for being	*Honor self first, to listen to the true intent of your soul. Your spirit/soul reminds you to aim for the sky, set your goals and stay on path step-by-step; for you are here for this blink of time to feed your soul and learn your lessons.*
Stomach	Your need to fill your voids	*Always create new cravings to enhance your hunger for life. Fill yourself up with lasting fulfillment.*
Urinary tract/system	Being fluid	*Flow with life; be flexible and adaptable.*
Voice	The spokesperson for your soul	*Always create closeness with your words. Share thoughts, words, and requests that are valuable and worthy of communicating.*

Thank You Notes

Thank you for your Gift of Family

Danny
Thank you with all my heart, incredible husband,
friend and soul mate, for supporting me on this and all my ventures.
The music and love in your heart and soul brought harmony
and love into my life. In you, God gave me the most beautiful light. Your
willingness to take your lessons to the extreme and share your gifts with me
and the world is amazing. Your story of courage and our healing work
together helped launch my career and this beautiful book.
Thanks for loving me!

~

Andy and Julia
You're the best! Thank you for always being my greatest teachers.
I am, and always will be, in awe of your insights and wisdom.
I am so proud of you both and I love you to infinity and beyond.
Julia's quote: What you say is what you do and
what you do is what you say!
Andy's quote: Whatever you practice right—you do right!

~

Khaki
Thank you, my spiritual healing pup and co-worker.
We're so glad you showed up at the pound
at just the right moment to rescue our family!
Your purpose is honored!

The Saul Family
Diane and Stanley, Perry, Penny, Alyssa, Andrea, Jake,
Howard, Gail, Lauren and Michael.

Thanks for your continual love and support throughout the years!
How blessed I am, Mom and Dad, to have been born into the most
incredible team of diversity, yet sharing the same message of love!
Your lessons—"Shoot For The Stars" and "You Can Do Anything"—
have always guided me. I am grateful and I love you!

~

The Kahn Family
Sue, Gary, Steve, Beth, Ben, Alex and Sara

Thanks for all your love and encouragement! Thanks, Mom, for being the
most wonderful mother-in-law and always supporting my journey!
Your openness in sharing your life's challenge was such a catalyst in this
book for great insights. I love you!

Thank you for your Gift of Talent

My Team of Writers and Editors

Mardeene Burr Mitchell

*Thank you for taking my life's work and making it sing in my voice
so the world can hear it.*
*I admire the way you crafted my message so authentically
to express my intent. Your ability to communicate the essence
of my soul on the page is remarkable.*
*Your devotion to this project all year long was amazing, even through
the wee hours of the night. I appreciate you so much, friend!*

Sue Robbins

*Thank you for all your loyal time, patience and feedback
as I was learning this new language of writing!
The ideas we bounced back and forth were so valuable
to the process and such a key in the beginning stages.
I am indebted to you!*

Ginger Schlanger

*How blessed I feel for the dual role that you have in my life.
Not only are you a dear friend but you are also
an extremely talented writer and editor.
I am grateful for your professional skills.
You did such a great job seeking out the heart of the experience
and helping bring it to life on the page!*

Stephanie Leontis

*I am so grateful that you are in my life almost every day
as one of my closest friends. I appreciate
you pitching in under extreme pressure
and pouring your heart and soul into this book.
Thank you for your considerable writing and editing talents!*

Janice Brown

*Thanks for showing up so willingly just when we needed you,
with your catcher's mitt on, to make such great last-minute
error "catches" before typesetting!
I am so grateful for your discerning eye
and for your enthusiastic response to my messages.*

246

Thank you for your Gift of Creativity
Your work is exceptional!

Mardeene Burr Mitchell, writer, mardeene@mindspring.com

Graffolio—Sue Knopf, design & layout, graffolio@centurytel.net

Dunn & Associates—Kathi Dunn, cover design, www.dunn-design.com

Susan Kendrick Writing—Susan Kendrick & Graham Van Dixhorn,
back cover copy, kendrick@cheqnet.net

YourWebPartner.com—Jay Fenello

Thanks for your Gift of Sharing
To the inspiring stars of the Gift of Taking:

I am so grateful to all of you for allowing me to share your stories
as a mirror to help so many others.
You are shining examples of the courage to change!

Danny, Andy, Julia, Stanley, Diane, Donna, Carmen,
Alice, Elisa, Bonnie S, Heshie, Brittany, Jay, Vito, Beverly,
Jodi, John, Tony, Michael, Lisa, Bonnie P., Deborah,
Sue, Beth, Ricky, Christopher, Cheryl, Penny, Tammy,
Leslie, Randi, Brad, Laura Beth and Andrew.

A very special thank you to Debbie S. for being the midwife
to help birth the six-day experience.

Thank you for your Gift of Trust
To all my treasured patients

Thank you for trusting me
with your most precious commodity—YOU!
How honored and blessed I feel
to have the privilege of all your
beautiful lessons and insights flowing through me.
These have been lessons well-shared!

Thank you for your Gift of Friendship

Sherrie Adir, The Stulak's, Tammy Hewlett,
The Fenello's, Trudy Brown and Frank Fenello, Donna Cochran, Kwajalyn
Sayers, Penny Jensen, Judy Keating, John Hilleary, and The Parker's—

Thanks for believing in me. Your support and encouragement has been a
staple through this journey. I love and appreciate all of you!

Carmen Hering—a special thank you for being the "catalyst" during
endless hours of recordings. I love and appreciate you!

Thank you for the Gift of Life

To Our Universe

Thank you for always supporting me every step of my path.
I vow to continually listen and align.
I now and always will remain in awe
of your creations as I remain in awe of,
and grateful for, my gift of life.

Thank you for your Gift of Vision

Jill,
I am so honored to have the privilege
of presenting your significant contribution to the world.
Thank you for entrusting me
with this grand mission.
What a exhilarating experience!
Your brilliant energy, one-pointed attention
and passion were unbelievable.
You have taught me so much
about blazing new trails with inner knowingness.
Your unerring intuition and clarity always
guided the project masterfully.
Most of all, what a pleasure to write, learn
and be with such a loving spirit and friend
and to be included in her magical world
of all people and all possibilities.

Mardeene

$\mathcal{I}$ am blessed with the PRIVILEGE of having powerful lessons flow through me revealing insights that so many are desiring to know, in ways that are accessible.

One thing that I know for certain—there is nothing new in life. Everything is revealed in the perfect time, order and sequence. We all desire the same—what's good in life—health, happiness, prosperity, etc. We search for evidence to reveal the obvious—what we so deserve. If it is presented in a way that makes sense to us, we get it and give ourselves permission to take it in and move forward. Then we overflow our expanded knowledge and experience, as our new value and worth for others to take once again.

We each are recycling our ways and thoughts to each other in search of our inner truth, sharing from each other's overflow.

Keep taking . . .

Enjoy all the information and insights you deem valuable within these pages—then overflow them as shared gifts for all.

Let us all grow and learn together.

Dr. Jill

Take love, Take it easy, Take it slow, Take a break, Take a breather, Take time out, Take care, Take five, Take charge, Take your time, Take a look, Take a bow, Take out, Take after, Take a breath, Take your turn, Take responsibility, Take control, Take a bite, Take it fast, Take a risk, Take a vacation, Take a trip, Take a tour, Take a journey, Take a class, Take a lesson, Take caution, Take a stretch, Take back what you said, Take a step, Take a moment, Take a mouthful, Take two, Take a piece, Take it lightly, Take a walk, Take credit, Take a bath, Take a shower, Take a swim, Take a cruise, Take a hike, Take a turn for the better, Take an interest, Take notice, Take a warning, Take a sign, Take a signal, Take Caution, Take Heed, Take up a hobby, Take note of, Take a taste, Take advantage, Take a load off you feet, Take help, Take it back, Take a hint, Take some, Take advice, Take suggestions, Take more, Take less, Take enough, Take plenty, Take a roll, Take regard, Take a look upon, Take a drive, Take a ride, Take your space, Take my hand, Take support, Take a clue, Take notice, Take a tip, Take direction, Take it in, Take a team, Take another, Take the rap, Take the blame, Take extra, Take love, Take happiness, Take your share, Take the entire package, Take note, Take offerings, Take turns, Take a chill, Take it to the limit, Take your fair share, Take your worth, Take ownership, Take exception to, Take offense at, Take possession, Take occupancy, Take a view, Take a second look, Do a double-take, Take a rest, Take this, Take that, Take it, Take everything, Take anything, Take something, Take a piece, Take a nap, Take the offer, Take a right, Take a left, Take the whole thing, Take donations, Take gifts, Take home pay, Take hand outs, Take lovingly, Take affection, Take your rights, Take your belongings, Take your stuff, Take it entirely, Take lessons, Take a step, Take after, Take up again, Take credit where credit is due, Take turns, Take up your heels, Take it upon yourself, Take in quest, Take in hand, Take a stride, Take a stroll, Take into consideration, Take into custody, Take into service, Take issue, Takes its toll, Take in life, Take lodgings, Taken as a whole, Taken back, Take-off, Take wing, Take you back, Take your breath away, Take your first breath, Take your last breath, Take your leave, Take your life back, Take into account, Simply take it, Take it lightly, Take it seriously, Take it away, Take it to the top, Take cover, Take note, Take a copy, Take an original, Take a peek, Take a flight, Take a trip, Take a vacation, Take a ride, Take a whirl, Take a shot at it, Take at face value, Take as read, Take a quick look, Take a glance, Take a glimpse, Take a rain check, Take a seat, Take a shine to, Take a softer line, Take a firm stance, Take a broad view, Take a chance on, Take a crack at, Take a deep breath, Take a dim view, Take a drop, Take a drink, Take a sip, Take a taste, Take a nibble, Take a fall, Take a fancy to, Take a gamble on, Take a new direction, Take account of, Take in air, Take advantage of, Take a stab at, Take a stand, Take a turn for the better, Take apart, Take as fact, Take for granted, Take a look at, Take a liking to, Take an oath, Take a small amount, Take a lot, Take it all, Take twice as much, Take your fair share, Take a spin, Take charge, Take it back, Take one, Take a load off your mind, Take a chance, Point well taken, You've got what it takes...

IT'S A TAKE!!!!!!!!!

Personal Notes

Personal Notes